To the Student

The best way to learn economics is to work lots of problems. This study guide contains numerous problems along with complete answers to the problems. To maximize the impact of your study time, use the following features of this study guide to solidify your overall understanding of the material and to enhance your performance on exams:

- **Chapter Outline.** Each chapter of the study guide begins with an overview (in condensed outline form) of the corresponding chapter in the textbook. Looking at the big picture is the best way to put things in prospective. *Study tip: Read the chapter outline before reading the corresponding text chapter, and again after reading it.*

- **Key Concepts.** Each chapter of the study guide summarizes the important principles, definitions, and concepts contained in the corresponding chapter in the textbook. *Study tip: Make sure you understand these concepts before attempting to work the problems.*

- **Questions.** Each chapter of the study guide has a section called "Questions." These are designed to help you master the concepts presented in the chapter. Answers to the questions are provided at the end of each study guide chapter. *Study tip: To maximize your grade, you should use the answers to check your own work instead of studying from the answers.*

- **Technical Problems.** Each chapter of the study guide has a section called "Technical Problems." These problems are designed to help you master the mechanics of working problems, as well as to learn to think about economics from an economist's perspective. Again, answers to the problems are provided at the end of each study guide chapter. *Study tip: To maximize your grade, you should use the answers to check your own work rather than attempt to study from the answers.*

- **Multiple Choice and True/False Questions.** Finally, each study guide chapter contains assorted multiple choice and true/false questions. *Study tip: After checking your answers, make sure you understand why the other options were not correct.*

- **Complete Answers.** As noted, the end of each study guide chapter contains detailed answers to the Questions and Technical Problems, as well as answers to the Multiple Choice and True/False Questions.

- **Internet Access.** Check out my personal homepage (http://php.indiana.edu/~mbaye) and my page at Irwin/McGraw-Hill (http://www.mhhe.com/economics/baye) for additional information, including errata for this study guide.

Study Guide

to accompany

Managerial Economics
and Business Strategy

Third Edition

Michael R. Baye
Indiana University

Irwin
McGraw-Hill

Boston   Burr Ridge, IL   Dubuque, IA   Madison, WI   New York   San Francisco   St. Louis
Bangkok   Bogotá   Caracas   Lisbon   London   Madrid
Mexico City   Milan   New Delhi   Seoul   Singapore   Sydney   Taipei   Toronto

McGraw-Hill Higher Education

A Division of The McGraw-Hill Companies

Study Guide to accompany
MANAGERIAL ECONOMICS AND BUSINESS STRATEGY

Copyright ©2000, 1997, 1994 by The McGraw-Hill Companies, Inc. All rights reserved.
Printed in the United States of America. The contents of, or parts thereof, may be reproduced for use with
MANAGERIAL ECONOMICS AND BUSINESS STRATEGY
Michael R. Baye
provided such reproductions bear copyright notice and may not be reproduced in
any form for any other purpose without permission of the publisher.

3 4 5 6 7 8 9 0 QPD/QPD 9 0 3 2 1 0

ISBN 0-07-228918-X

http://www.mhhe.com

Contents

Chapter 1
The Fundamentals of Managerial Economics

Chapter 1 at a Glance

Key Concepts: Chapter 1

1.   A manager is a person who directs resources in order to achieve a stated goal.

2.   Economics is the science of making decisions in the presence of scarce resources.

3.   Managerial economics is the study of how to direct scarce resources in the means that most efficiently achieves a managerial goal.

4.   Opportunity cost refers to the cost of the explicit and implicit resources that are foregone when a decision is made.

5.   Economic profit is the difference between the total revenue and total opportunity cost.

6.   Profits signal resource holders where resources are most highly valued by society.

7.   The present value (PV) of a future value (FV) received n years in the future is

$$PV = \frac{FV}{(1+i)^n}$$

where i is the guaranteed (risk-free) rate of interest.

8.   When the interest rate is i, the present value of a stream of payments of FV_1, FV_2,...FV_n is

$$PV = \sum_{t=1}^{n} \frac{FV_t}{(1+i)^t}.$$

9.   The net present value of a project that costs C_0 dollars today and that generates income of FV_1 one year in the future, FV_2 two years in the future, and so on for n years, is given by

$$NPV = \frac{FV_1}{(1+i)^1} + \frac{FV_2}{(1+i)^2} + \frac{FV_3}{(1+i)^3} + \cdots + \frac{FV_n}{(1+i)^n} - C_0.$$

Managers should accept projects that have a positive net present value, and reject ones that have negative net present values.

10.   Maximizing profits means maximizing the value of the firm, which is the present value of all future profits.

11. If the growth rate in profits is less than the interest rate, and both are constant, then maximizing the present value of all future profits is the same as maximizing current profits.

12. The marginal (or incremental) benefit (MB) of the managerial control variable, Q, is the change in total benefits arising from a change in the control variable:

$$MB = \frac{\Delta B}{\Delta Q}.$$

13. The marginal (or incremental) cost (MC) of the managerial control variable, Q, is the change in total costs arising from a change in the control variable:

$$MC = \frac{\Delta C}{\Delta Q}.$$

14. In order to maximize net benefits, the managerial control variable should be increased up to the point where marginal benefits equal marginal costs. This level of the managerial control variable corresponds to the level where marginal net benefits (MNB) are zero; nothing more can be gained by further changes in the managerial control variable.

15. When the control variable is infinitely divisible, the slope of a total value curve at a given point is the marginal value at that point. In particular, the slope of the total benefit curve at a given Q is the marginal benefit of that level of Q. The slope of the total cost curve at a given Q is the marginal cost of that level of Q. The slope of the net benefit curve at a given Q is the marginal net benefit of that level of Q.

16. Since the slope of a function is the derivative of the function, the derivative of a given function is the marginal value of that function. For example:

$$MB = \frac{dB(Q)}{dQ}$$

$$MC = \frac{dC(Q)}{dQ}$$

$$MNB = \frac{dN(Q)}{dQ}.$$

17. Incremental (or yes or no) decisions are profitable whenever incremental revenues exceed incremental costs.

Questions: Chapter 1

1. List the six basic principles of effective management.

   a.

   b.

   c.

   d.

   e.

   f.

2. Joe faced the following options: (a) pay $5,000 in tuition to attend classes at Econ Tech; (b) work as a fry cook for $4,000; or (c) work as a waiter at an elite restaurant and earn $10,000. What is Joe's opportunity cost of attending classes at Econ Tech?

3. What sources of rivalry always exist in markets serviced by two or more buyers and two or more sellers?

   a.

   b.

   c.

4.   What sources of rivalry always exist in markets serviced by a single seller and two or more buyers?

       a.

       b.

5.   a.   State the formula for computing the present value (PV) of a future amount (FV) received in n years when the interest rate is i.

       b.   Looking at the present value formula, what happens to the present value when the interest rate increases (that is, as i increases)?

       c.   Looking at the present value formula, what happens to the present value when the future amount is received farther into the future (that is, as n increases)?

       d.   Looking at the present value formula, what happens to the present value when the amount to be received in the future increases (that is, as FV increases)?

6.   Explain, in words, the condition required for a manager to maximize the net benefits derived from the use of a managerial control variable.

Technical Problems: Chapter 1

1.   The manager of an office supply company is contemplating the purchase of a new copier, which will cost $50,000 and has a useful life of 3 years. The copier will save the firm $20,000 in year one, $20,000 in the second year, and $10,000 in the third year. The machine can be re-sold at the end of three years to a junk dealer for $5,000. Alternatively, the manager can invest the $50,000 at a guaranteed interest rate of 5%. To maximize profits, should the manager purchase the copier or invest the money at 5%?

2.   Delta, Inc. is expected to grow at an annual rate of 3 percent for the foreseeable future. The current profits of Delta are 1,000 dollars. What is the value of the firm (the present value of all present and future earnings) assuming the market interest rate is 6%?

3.　　A firm hired an economist to evaluate the benefits and costs of increasing the number of square feet (S) of inventory space. The results of the study are as follows:

$$B(S) = 4{,}000S - S^2$$

$$C(S) = S^2$$

Your assistant informs you that marginal benefits are MB = 4,000 - 2S and marginal costs are MC = 2S.

a.　　How many square feet should be added to maximize the net benefits?

b.　　What are the maximum net benefits?

c.　　How many square feet should be added to maximize total benefits?

d.　　What are the maximum total benefits?

4. The manager of a software company seeks to maximize profits by producing the profit-maximizing level of output (Q). The total benefits (revenues) and costs for various levels of output are summarized below, and are given in millions of dollars. Complete the table, and answer the accompanying questions.

(1)	(2)	(3)	(4)	(5)	(6)	(7)
Q	B	C	B - C	MB	MC	MNB
0	0	0		--	--	--
1	20	10				
2	38	25				
3	54	41				
4	58	59				
5	50	79				

a. What level of output maximizes net benefits?

b. What is the relation between marginal benefits and marginal cost at this level of output?

c. What would happen if the manager attempted to maximize total benefits?

d. Are marginal benefits zero when total benefits are maximized? Why or why not?

8

5. Your research department has estimated the total benefits (revenues) and costs of producing output (Q) to be

$$B(Q) = 8000Q - 3Q^2$$

and

$$C(Q) = Q^2,$$

so that MB = 8000 - 6Q and MC = 2Q.

a. What level of Q maximizes profits?

b. What is marginal revenue at this level of Q?

c. What is the maximum level of profits?

6. Answer the following questions based on Exhibit 1-1

a. Curve A is the _____ curve.

b. Curve B is the _____ curve.

c. The slope of line C is the _____ of 50 units.

d. The slope of line D is the _____ of 50 units.

e. The length of line segment E represents the _____.

f. The marginal benefit of using 50 units of the managerial control variable is _____.

9

g. Assuming 50 units maximizes net benefits, the value of costs at point F is _____.

h. The net benefit of using 50 units of the managerial control variable is_____.

i. The marginal net benefit of using 50 units of the managerial control variable is _____.

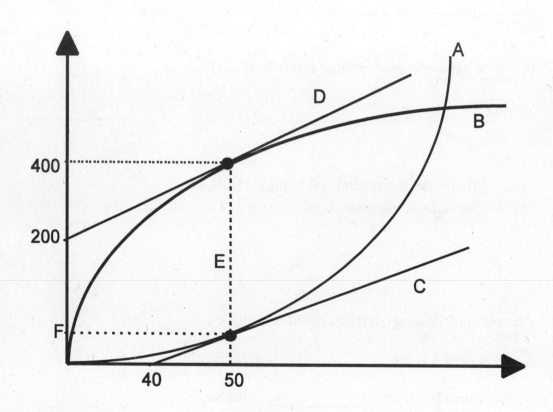

Exhibit 1-1

7.   You are the manager of a small print shop, and are contemplating the purchase of a new computer network designed to enhance efficiency.

a.   Complete the following table.

	Current Situation	If Purchase the Network	Incremental Revenues and Costs
Total Revenue	$100,000	$101,000	
Variable Cost	40,000	30,000	
Direct Fixed Costs	50,000	59,000	
Indirect Fixed Costs	10,000	10,000	
Profit			

b.   Should you purchase the new computer network? Explain

Multiple Choice and True/False Questions: Chapter 1

1. In general, as firms leave an industry:
    a. accounting profits fall
    b. economic profits increase
    c. economic profits decline
    d. prices fall

2. Scarce resources are ultimately allocated toward the production of goods most wanted by society because of the:
    a. goal of firms to maximize profits
    b. fact that they are most efficiently utilized in these areas
    c. demand of consumers for inexpensive goods and services
    d. benevolence of managers of firms.

3. The opportunity cost of receiving ten dollars in the future as opposed to getting that ten dollars today is:
    a. foregone interest that could be earned if you had the money today
    b. the value of the goods and services that money can purchase
    c. the relative value of that money in regard to total income
    d. the level of wealth for each individual and the effect an additional ten dollars will have on wealth

4. What is the present value of receiving ten dollars one year from now, given that the interest rate is 5 percent?
    a. $ 9.50
    b. $10.05
    c. $ 9.52
    d. $ 9.77

5. If you put $1,000 in a savings account at an interest rate of 7%, how much money will you have in one year?
    a. $1,007
    b. $1,070
    c. $934.58
    d. $930

6. If the interest rate is 7%, the present value of $1,000 received 1 year from now would be:
    a. $1,007
    b. $1,070
    c. $934.58
    d. $930

7. A firm will have constant profits of $10 per year at the end of each year for the next two years and zero profits thereafter. If the interest rate is six percent, what is the value of the firm?
    a. $18.33
    b. $20.00
    c. $40
    d. $34.65

8. Suppose the interest rate is five percent, the expected growth rate of the firm is two percent, and the firm is expected to continue forever. If current profits are $100, what is the value of the firm?
    a. $3,100
    b. $3,000
    c. $2,650
    d. $3,500

9. To maximize net benefits, a manager should continue to increase the managerial control variable until:
    a. total benefits equal total cost
    b. net benefits are zero
    c. marginal benefits equal marginal cost
    d. average cost equals average benefits

10. Economic profits play an important role in a market economy because
    a. they signal where resources are most highly valued
    b. are used to pay workers
    c. are used to pay taxes
    d. provide workers an incentive to work hard

11. The present value of $100 received in seven years, if the interest rate is 5%, is:
    a. $100/(0.07)^5$
    b. $100/(1 + .07)^5$
    c. $100 (1 + .07)^5$
    d. none of the above

12. If the marginal net benefits of Q are positive, it is profitable
    a. to increase Q.
    b. to decrease Q.
    c. to stay at that level of Q.
    d. all of the above

13. Maximizing total benefits results in maximizing net benefits when:
   a. costs are zero.
   b. costs are rising.
   c. costs are rising and then falling.
   d. none of the above.

14. True or False: The marginal benefit curve is the slope of the total benefits curve.

15. True or False: The slope of the marginal net benefit curve is horizontal where MB = MC.

16. True or False: The difference in the slope of the marginal benefit curve and the marginal cost curve is maximized at the optimal level of Q.

17. True or False: The best way to learn economics is to highlight the important material in the text and then continue reading the highlighted material until you understand it.

18. True or False: The greater the interest rate, the greater the present value of a given future amount.

19. True or False: When total benefits are falling, marginal benefits are negative.

20. True or False: When total costs are rising, marginal costs are negative.

Answers to Questions: Chapter 1

.1.   a.   Identify Goals and Constraints

       b.   Recognize the Nature and Importance of Profits

       c.   Understand Incentives

       d.   Understand Markets

       e.   Recognize the Time Value of Money

       f.   Use Marginal Analysis

2. $15,000. Joe's opportunity cost of going to college includes both the explicit cost ($5,000) plus the implicit cost ($10,000) of his next best alternative. In other words, by choosing to go to college Joe gives up the opportunity to spend $5,000 of his money on other goods or services, and he also gives up a $10,000 job. Notice that the $4,000 job is irrelevant since he cannot work at both jobs at the same time; the relevant implicit cost is the best of the mutually exclusive alternatives.

3.   a.   consumer-consumer rivalry

     b.   consumer-producer rivalry

     c.   producer-producer rivalry

4.   a.   consumer-consumer rivalry

     b.   consumer-producer rivalry

5.   a.   The present value formula is:

$$PV = \frac{FV}{(1 + i)^n}$$

     b.   The present value falls.

     c.   The present value falls.

     d.   The present value rises.

6.   To maximize net benefits, a manager should continue to use a control variable up to the point where the marginal benefits equal the marginal cost.

Answers to Technical Problems: Chapter 1

1. By purchasing the copier, the firm effectively earns $20,000 in year 1, $20,000 in year 2, and $15,000 in year three (the $10,000 cost savings plus the $5,000 from the junk dealer). Thus the present value of benefits of buying the copier is

$$PV = \frac{20,000}{1.05} + \frac{20,000}{1.05^2} + \frac{15,000}{1.05^3} = \$50,145.77.$$

Since this present value exceeds the cost of the copier ($50,000), the manager maximizes profits by purchasing the copier instead of investing the $50,000 at 5%. In other words, the net present value is positive: $NPV = PV - C_0 = \$50,145.77 - \$50,000 = \$145.77$.

2. Using equation 1-5 of the textbook, we see that

$$PV_{FIRM} = (\$1,000) \left[\frac{1 + .06}{.06 - .03} \right] = (\$1,000)(35.33333) = \$35,333.33.$$

3. a. Equating MB and MC yields $4,000 - 2S = 2S$. Solving this equation for S reveals that net benefits are maximized by adding $S^* = 1,000$ additional square feet of inventory space.

    b. $NB(S^*) = B(S^*) - C(S^*) = 4,000(1,000) - (1,000)^2 - (1,000)^2 = 2,000,000$.

    c. To maximize total benefits, set marginal benefits equal to zero:

    $$MB(S) = 4,000 - 2S = 0.$$

    Solving for S yields $S^* = 2,000$.

    d. $B(S^*) = 4,000(2,000) - (2,000)^2 = 4,000,000$.

4.   The completed table is as follows:

(1)	(2)	(3)	(4)	(5)	(6)	(7)
Q	B	C	B - C	MB	MC	MNB
0	0	0	0	--	--	--
1	20	10	10	20	10	10
2	38	25	13	18	15	3
3	54	41	13	16	16	0
4	58	59	-1	4	18	-14
5	50	79	-29	-8	20	-28

a.   2 or 3 units of output.

b.   Marginal benefits equal marginal cost at 3 units of output.

c.   The firm would produce 4 units and make a loss of $1 million.

d.   No. this is because the managerial control variable is discrete, not continuous.

5.   a.   Equate MB and MC to get $8,000 - 6Q = 2Q$. Solving for Q yields $Q^* = 1,000$.

b.   Marginal revenue, in this case is simply marginal benefits. At $Q^* = 1,000$, we have $MB(Q^*) = 8000 - 6(1,000) = 2,000$.

c.   Maximum profits, in this case, are $B(Q^*) - C(Q^*) = 8,000(1,000) - 3(1,000)^2 - (1,000)^2 = \$4,000,000$.

6.   a.   total cost

b.   total benefit

c.   marginal cost

d.   marginal benefit

e. net benefits of 50 units

f. 4, since the slope of line D is (400 - 200)/50 = 4.

g. 40. We know this because MB = MC at 50 units of output, and from part f. MB = 4. Thus, the slope of line C must be 4. This implies F/(50 - 40) = 4. Solving for F gives us F = 40.

h. 400 - 40 = 360.

i. 0.

7. a. The completed table looks like this:

	Current Situation	If Purchase the Network	Incremental Revenues and Costs
Total Revenue	$100,000	$101,000	$1,000
Variable Cost	40,000	30,000	(10,000)
Direct Fixed Costs	50,000	59,000	9,000
Indirect Fixed Costs	10,000	10,000	0
Profit	0	$2,000	$2,000

b. You should purchase the new computer network because the incremental revenues of $1,000 exceed the incremental costs of $-1,000. In other words, you will reduce your costs by $1,000 by purchasing the new network, and you also generate an additional $1,000 in revenues, for a total increase in profit of $2,000.

18

Answers to Multiple Choice and True/False Questions:
Chapter 1

1. b
2. a
3. a
4. c
5. b
6. c
7. a
8. d
9. c
10. a
11. d
12. a
13. a
14. True
15. False; MNB = 0 and the slope is negative
16. False; net benefits are maximized
17. False; work problems!
18. False; the lower the PV.
19. True
20. False; they are positive.

Chapter 2
Market Forces: Demand and Supply

Chapter 2 at a Glance

Key Concepts: Chapter 2

1. If the price of a good falls and all other things remain the same, the quantity demanded of the good rises.

2. The market demand curve indicates the quantity consumers are willing and able to purchase at each possible price, holding the prices of related goods, income, advertising, and other variables constant.

3. Changes in the price of good X lead to a change in the quantity demanded of good X. This corresponds to a movement along a given demand curve. Changes in variables other than the price of good X, such as income or the price of good Y, lead to a change in demand. This corresponds to a shift of the entire demand curve.

4. Good X is a normal good if an increase (a decrease) in income leads to an increase (a decrease) in the demand for good X.

5. Good X is an inferior good if an increase (a decrease) in income leads to a decrease (an increase) in the demand for good X.

6. Good X is a substitute for good Y if an increase (a decrease) in the price of good Y leads to an increase (a decrease) in the demand for good X.

7. Good X is a complement to good Y if an increase (a decrease) in the price of good Y leads to a decrease (an increase) in the demand for good X.

8. The demand function for good X describes how much of good X will be purchased at alternative prices of good X and related goods, alternative levels of income, and alternative values of other variables that affect demand. Formally, let Q_x^d represent the quantity consumed of good X, let P_x be the price of good X, P_y the price of a related good, M income, and let H denote the value of any other variable that affects demand. Then the demand function for good X may be written as

$$Q_x^d = f(P_x, P_y, M, H).$$

The variable H might represent the level of advertising; or it might represent a variable such as rainfall that influences the demand for products such as umbrellas.

9.   Demand is linear if Q_x^d is a linear function of prices, income, and other variables that influence demand. The following equation is an example of a linear demand function:

$$Q_x^d = \alpha_o + \alpha_x P_x + \alpha_y P_y + \alpha_M M + \alpha_H H.$$

The α_i's are fixed numbers that are given to the manager.

10.   Consumer surplus is the value consumers get from a good but do not have to pay for. It provides a measure of how much extra consumers would be willing to pay for a given quantity of the good. Geometrically, consumer surplus is the area above the price paid for a good but below the demand curve.

11.   The market supply curve indicates the total quantity all producers in a competitive market would produce at each price, holding input prices, technology, and other variables that affect supply constant.

12.   As the price of a good rises and other things remain the same, the quantity supplied of the good rises.

13.   Changes in the price of a good lead to a change in the quantity supplied of the good. This corresponds to a movement along a given supply curve. Changes in variables other than the price of the good, such as input prices or a change in technology, lead to changes in supply. This corresponds to a shift in the entire supply curve.

14.   The supply function of a good describes how much of the good will be produced at alternative prices of the good, alternative prices of inputs, and alternative values of other variables that affect supply. Formally, let Q_x^s represent the quantity supplied of a good. Let P_x be the price of the good, W the price of an input (such as the wage rate on labor), P_r the price of technologically related good, and let H denote the value of some other variable that affects supply. Then the supply function for good X may be written as

$$Q_x^s = f(P_x, P_r, W, H).$$

The variable H might summarize the existing technology; or it might represent a variable such as rainfall that influences the supply of agricultural products.

15.   Supply is linear if Q_x^s is a linear function of variables that influence supply. The following equation is representative of a linear supply function:

$$Q_x^s = \beta_0 + \beta_x P_x + \beta_r P_r + \beta_w W + \beta_H H.$$

The β_i's represent fixed numbers that are given to the manager.

23

16. Producers surplus is the amount received by producers in excess of the amount necessary to induce them to produce the good. Geometrically, producer surplus is the area above the supply curve but below the market price of the good.

17. Equilibrium in a competitive market is determined by the intersection of the market demand and supply curves. The equilibrium price is the price that equates quantity demanded with quantity supplied. Mathematically, if $Q^d(P)$ and $Q^s(P)$ represent the quantity demanded and supplied when the price is P, then the equilibrium price, P^e, is the price such that

$$Q^d(P^e) = Q^s(P^e).$$

The equilibrium quantity is simply $Q^d(P^e)$ (or equivalently, $Q^s(P^e)$).

18. A price ceiling is the maximum legal price that can be charged in a market.

19. The full economic price (P^F) equals the dollar amount paid to a firm under a price ceiling (P^c), plus the non-pecuniary price paid by waiting in line.

20. A floor price is the minimum legal price that can be charged in a market.

Questions: Chapter 2

1. Explain the difference between a change in demand and a change in quantity demanded.

Δ in demand $\Rightarrow$ Shift of the entire Demand curve. cause by something else than ΔP

Δ qty demanded $\Rightarrow$ movement along the D curve cause by ΔP

2. List 5 demand shifters, and explain the direction in which they shift demand.

a. Income — Normal $\ell I \uparrow \Rightarrow D_x \uparrow$
   unferior if $I \downarrow \Rightarrow D_x \uparrow$

b. Price of related good. — Substitute $P_y \uparrow \Rightarrow D_x \uparrow$
   — complement $P_x \uparrow \Rightarrow D_x \downarrow$ ✓

c. Advertisement. $\Rightarrow \uparrow D$
   or $\uparrow P$ ($\uparrow$ mq. demanded) ✓

d. Consumer's expectation if P is believe to be cheaper
   to morre $P_{todos} \downarrow$ ✓

e. population   as POP $\uparrow \Rightarrow D \uparrow$ ✓

3. What is consumer surplus?

price that some customer would be
willing to pay for a product but
do not have to ✓

4. Explain the difference between a change in supply and a change in quantity supplied.

Δ Supply $\Rightarrow$ shift of Supply curve (Not due to ΔP)

Δq supplier $\Rightarrow$ movement along the S curve
   caus by ΔP

5. List 5 supply shifters, and explain the direction in which they shift supply.

a. technology + government regulation

b. tax   -incise → excuse
          -ad torem. valoren 8

c. price of input. ✓ →

d. producer expectation → ↓ believe cheaper too

e. substitute in production
   P more π when dony Y
   → shift X → Y
firms

6. What is producer surplus?

P some producer would be willing to charge but do not have to. (reserve p.u.)

7. What determines the price and quantity of goods available in a free market?

interaction between S and D

8. a. What is a price ceiling?

legally max P a product can be charged

b. What effect does an effective price ceiling have on the market?

creates a shortage and a new opp price based on opp cost
qs < qp

high price economic

qs qp

26

9. a. What is a price floor?

legally min price a product can be charged

b. What effect does an effective price floor have on the market?

creates a surplus

10. Exhibit 2-1 shows the market supply and demand curves for a good. Based on this diagram, answer the following questions:

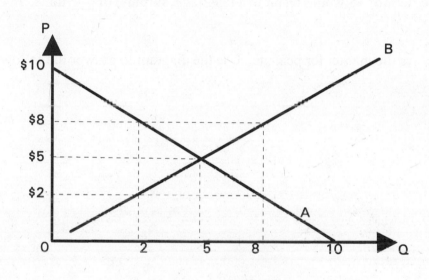

Exhibit 2-1

a. Curve ___A___ is the demand curve.

b. Curve ___B___ is the supply curve.

c. The equilibrium price is ___$5___.

d. The equilibrium quantity is ___5___.

e. At the point of equilibrium, consumer surplus is ___12.5___ dollars.

27

f. At the point of equilibrium, producer surplus is __12.5__ dollars.

g. A price ceiling of $2 would result in quantity demanded of __8__ units.

h. A price ceiling of $2 would result in quantity supplied of __2__ units.

i. A price ceiling of $2 would result in a ((shortage), surplus) of __6__ units.

j. A price ceiling of $2 would result in a full economic price of __8__ dollars.

k. A price floor of $8 would result in quantity demanded of __2__ units.

l. A price floor of $8 would result in quantity supplied of __8__ units.

m. A price floor of $8 would result in a (shortage, (surplus)) of __6__ units.

11. Exhibit 2-2 shows the market for peanuts. Use the diagram to answer the following questions.

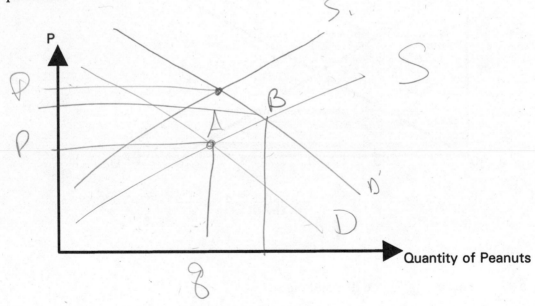

Exhibit 2-2

a. Draw the market equilibrium, and label the equilibrium point A.

b. Assume peanuts are an inferior good. Illustrate in the above graph what would happen to the market for peanuts during a recession (label the new equilibrium point B).

28

c. Now suppose that, in addition to the recession, a peanut blight destroys much of the nation's peanut crop. Use your diagram to show what must happen to the equilibrium price as a result of the recession and peanut blight.

P↑ undetermine for g *S↓*

Technical Problems: Chapter 2

1. The demand for company X's product is given by

$$Q_x^d = 12 - 3P_x - 4P_y + 1M + 2A_x$$

where A_x represents the amount of advertising on good X, P_x is the price of good X, P_y is the price of good Y, and M is income. Good X sells at \$2 per unit, good Y sells for \$1 per unit, the company utilizes 2 units of advertising, and consumer income is \$10.

a. How much of good X is purchased by consumers?

12 − 6 − 4 + 10 + 4 = 2 + 10 + 4 = 16 ✓

b. Are goods X and Y substitutes or complements? ✓

c. Is good X a normal or inferior good?

d. Find an equation for the demand curve and the inverse demand curve.

Q = 12 − 3P − 4 + 10 + 4
= 8 + 10 + 4 − 3P
Q = 22 − 3P ✓

P = 1/3 Q − 22/3 ✓

29

2. The supply function for good X is given by

$$Q_x^s = 20 + 2P_x - P_w,$$

where P_x represents the price of good X and P_w is the price of an input. Good X sells for $4 per unit and that the price of the input is $1.

a. How many units of good X are produced?

$$Q = 20 + 8 - 1 = 27 \checkmark$$

b. Find an equation for the supply curve and the inverse supply curve.

$$Q = 20 + 2P - 1 \checkmark$$
$$Q = 19 + 2P$$
$$P = \frac{Q}{2} - \frac{19}{2} \checkmark$$

3. Suppose the market demand and supply curves are given by $Q^d = 20 - 3P$ and $Q^s = P$, respectively.

a. Determine the equilibrium price.

$$20 - 3P = P$$
$$20 = 4P$$
$$P = 5 \checkmark$$

b. Determine the equilibrium quantity.

$$Q = 20 - 15 = 5$$
$$Q = 5 \checkmark$$

30

4.   Given the market demand and supply curves in problem 3 above, if the government imposes a price ceiling of $2:

$Q^d = 20 - 3P$
$Q^s = P$

a.   Calculate the magnitude of the resulting shortage.

$Q^d = 20 - 6 = 14$
$Q^s = 2$
    Shortage $= 12$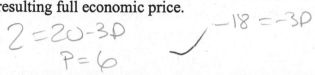

b.   Calculate the resulting full economic price.

$2 = 20 - 3P$
$P = 6$ $-18 = -3P$

5.   Given the market demand and supply curves in problem 3 above, if the government imposes a price floor of $6: $P = 6$

$Q^d = 20 - 3P$
$Q^s = P$

a.   Calculate the magnitude of the resulting surplus.

$Q^d = 20 - 18 = 2$
$Q^s = 6$
        Surplus $= 4$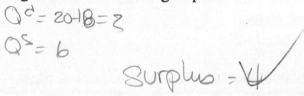

b.   What is the total cost to the government of buying the surplus?

        $4 \times 6 = 24$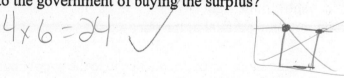

31

Multiple Choice and True/False Questions: Chapter 2

1. The law of supply states that, holding other things constant:
   a. as price rises, supply will rise
   b. as price rises, supply will decline
   c. as price falls, quantity supplied rises
   d. as price falls, quantity supplied declines

2. For a normal good, a decrease in income will lead to:
   a. a movement up the demand curve
   b. a leftward shift of the demand curve
   c. a rightward shift of the demand curve
   d. a movement down the demand curve.

3. If good Y is a substitute for good X, then a rise in the price of good X will result in
   a. a decrease in the demand for good Y
   b. a decrease in the demand for good X
   c. an increase in the demand for good X
   d. an increase in the demand for good Y

4. Which of the following pairs of goods are probably complements?
   a. guns and butter
   b. jelly beans and licorice
   c. steak and chicken
   d. potato chips and water

5. For a textbook publisher, an increase in the price of paper will cause the supply curve to:
   a. create consumer surplus
   b. shift to the left
   c. shift to the right
   d. become parallel to the price axis

6. A decline in an input price will cause the supply curve to:
   a. shift to the left
   b. shift to the right
   c. intersect demand at a higher price
   d. rotate counter clockwise

7. The maximum legal price that can be charged in a market is:
    a. a price ceiling
    b. the full economic price
    c. producer surplus
    d. a price floor

8. If comic books are inferior goods, what would happen to price and quantity during an economic boom?
    a. price would increase and quantity decrease
    b. price and quantity would both increase
    c. price and quantity would both decrease
    d. price would decrease and quantity increase

9. Which of the following is not a demand shifter?
    a. the price of substitutes.
    b. consumer income.
    c. the level of advertising.
    d. the price of complements.
    e. the price of the good

10. Producer surplus
    a. is the value consumers get from a supplier.
    b. is the value consumers do not pay because of a discount by supplier.
    c. is the value consumers get from a good but do not pay for.
    d. none of the above

11. True or False: The minimum wage is an example of a price ceiling.

12. True or False: If demand increases and supply decreases, the equilibrium price will rise and the quantity will fall.

13. True or False: If demand increases and supply increases, the equilibrium price will rise and the quantity will rise.

14. True or False: If supply and demand both decline, the equilibrium quantity will fall.

15. True or False: If steak is a normal good, then an increase in consumer income would result in an increase in the price of steak.

16. True or False: Price ceilings generally help consumers by allowing them to purchase the amount they want at a low price.

33

17. True or False: Prices below the equilibrium level result in shortages, while prices above equilibrium result in a surplus.

18. True or False: Higher prices of movies tend to reduce demand, and therefore lead to a lower equilibrium price of movie tickets.

Answers to Questions: Chapter 2

1. A change in quantity demanded is a movement along a given demand curve, and is caused by a change in the price of the good. A change in demand is a shift in the entire demand curve, and is caused by a change in a demand shifter.

2. a. Income. Increases (decreases) in income shift the demand for normal goods to the right (left). Increases (decreases) in income shift the demand for inferior goods to the left (right).

   b. Prices of related goods. An increase (decrease) in the price of a substitute shifts demand to the right (left). An increase (decrease) in the price of a complement shifts demand to the left (right).

   c. Advertising and consumer tastes. Changes that increase consumer desire to purchase the good shifts demand to the right. Changes that reduce consumer desire to purchase the good shifts demand to the left.

   d. Population. Generally, a rise in the size of the population shifts demand to the right.

   e. Consumer expectations. Expectations of higher (lower) future prices shift the current demand for a good to the right (left).

3. Consumer surplus represents the value consumers get from a good but do not have to pay for.

4. A change in quantity supplied is a movement along a given supply curve, and is caused by a change in the price of the good. A change in supply is a shift in the entire supply curve, and is caused by a change in a supply shifter.

5. a. Input prices. Higher (lower) input prices shift supply to the left (right).

    b. Technology or government regulations. Advances in technology or reductions in government regulations shift supply to the right.

    c. Number of firms. Increases (decreases) in the number of firms servicing a competitive market shifts supply to the right (left).

    d. Excise and ad valorem taxes. Increases (decreases) in these taxes reduce (increase) supply. Excise taxes are per unit taxes, and thus shift the supply curve upward by the amount of the tax. Ad valorem taxes are percentage taxes, and therefore rotate the supply curve leftward (making it steeper).

    e. Producer expectations. If producers expect prices to be higher (lower) in the future, current supply will decline (increase).

6. Producer surplus is the amount producers receive in excess of the amount necessary to induce them to produce the good.

7. The price and quantity of goods available in a free market are determined by the forces of supply and demand. More precisely, the price is determined by the intersection of the market supply and demand curves -- that price such that quantity demanded equals quantity supplied.

8. a. A price ceiling is the maximum legal price that can be charged for a good.

    b. An effective price ceiling makes the price artificially low, thereby reducing quantity supplied and increasing quantity demanded. The result is a shortage of the good.

9. a. A price floor is the minimum legal price than can be paid for a good.

    b. An effective price floor makes the price artificially high, thereby increasing the quantity supplied and decreasing quantity demanded. The result is a surplus of the good.

10. a. A

    b. B

c. $5

d.   5 units

e. $12.5. Compute this as 1/2 times the base quantity (5) times the height (10 - 5).

f. $12.5 Compute this as 1/2 times the base quantity (5) times the height (5 - 0).

g.   8

h.   2

i.   Shortage of 6 units

j. $8

k.   2

l.   8

m.   Surplus of 6 units.

11.   a.   The initial equilibrium is at point A in Exhibit 2-3.

b.   Since peanuts are an inferior good, declining income during a recession shifts demand to the right, resulting in a new equilibrium at point B in Exhibit 2-3.

c.   A peanut blight shifts supply to the left. Notice that regardless of how far it shifts (to point C or D), the new equilibrium price is higher in Exhibit 2-3. Quantity may rise, fall, or stay the same.

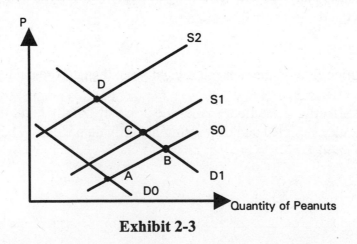

Exhibit 2-3

Answers to Technical Problems: Chapter 2

1.   a.   16 units, since $12 - 3(2) - 4(1) + 10 + 2(2) = 16$.

      b.   Complements, since the coefficient of P_y is a negative number (-4). This means an \$1 increase in the price of good Y decreases the demand for good X by 4 units.

      c.   Normal, since the coefficient of M is a positive number (1). This means a \$1 increase in income increases the demand for good X by 1 unit.

      d.   The demand curve is $Q_x^d = 12 - 3P_x - 4(1) + 10 + 2(2) = 22 - 3P_x$. The inverse demand curve is thus $P_x = 22/3 - Q_x^d/3$.

2.   a.   27 units, since $20 + 2(4) - 1 = 27$.

      b.   The supply curve is $Q_x^s = 20 + 2P_x - 1 = 19 + 2P_x$. Solving for P_x gives us the equation for the inverse supply curve: $P_x = Q_x^s/2 - 19/2$.

3.   a.   Set $Q^d = Q^s$ and solve to get $P = 5$.

      b.   Plug $P = 5$ into the demand (or supply) function to get $Q = 5$.

4.   a.   When $P = 2$, quantity demanded is $Q^d = 20 - 3(2) = 14$ units, while quantity supplied is $Q^s = 2$. Thus, there is a shortage of 12 units.

      b.   Plug P^F into the demand function and set this equal to the 2 units available under the ceiling: $2 = 20 - 3P^F$. Solving gives us the $P^F = \$6$. Notice that this is higher than the original equilibrium price.

5.   a.   Notice that at a price floor of \$6, quantity demanded by consumers is $20 - 3(6) = 2$ units. Producers will produce $Q^s = 6$ units at this price. Hence, there is a surplus of 4 units.

      b.   \$24, since it buys 4 units at a price of \$6 per unit.

Answers to Multiple Choice and True/False Questions: Chapter 2

1. d
2. b
3. d
4. d
5. b
6. b
7. a
8. c
9. e
10. d
11. False
12. False; quantity is indeterminant
13. False; price is indeterminant
14. True
15. True
16. False; they create shortages and raise the full economic price
17. True
18. False; higher prices reduce quantity demanded, which is a movement along a given demand curve.

Chapter 3
Quantitative Demand Analysis

Chapter 3 at a Glance

Key Concepts: Chapter 3

1. The elasticity of variable G with respect to variable S, denoted $E_{G,S}$, is defined as the percentage change in variable G that results from a given percentage change in variable S. In other words,

$$E_{G,S} = \frac{\%\Delta G}{\%\Delta S}.$$

2. If the variable G depends on S according to the functional relationship G = f(S), then the elasticity of G with respect to S may be found using calculus:

$$E_{G,S} = \frac{dG}{dS} \cdot \frac{S}{G}.$$

3. The own price elasticity of demand for good X is defined as

$$E_{Q_x,P_x} = \frac{\%\Delta Q_x^d}{\%\Delta P_x}.$$

4. Demand is said to be elastic if the absolute value of the own price elasticity is greater than one:

$$\left| E_{Q_x,P_x} \right| > 1.$$

5. Demand is said to be inelastic if the absolute value of the own price elasticity is less than one:

$$\left| E_{Q_x,P_x} \right| < 1.$$

6. Demand is said to be unitary elastic if the absolute value of the own price elasticity is equal to one:

$$\left| E_{Q_x,P_x} \right| = 1.$$

7. If demand is elastic, an increase (a decrease) in price will lead to a decrease (an increase) in total revenue. If demand is inelastic, an increase (a decrease) in price will lead to an increase (a decrease) in total revenue. Finally, total revenue is maximized at the point where demand is unitary elastic.

8.   Demand is perfectly elastic if the own price elasticity of demand is infinite in absolute value.

9.   Demand is perfectly inelastic if the own price elasticity of demand is zero.

10.   The cross price elasticity of demand between goods X and Y is defined as

$$\frac{\frac{Q_1-Q_0}{\overline{Q}} \times \overline{P}}{P_1 \stackrel{=}{\scriptstyle ?} P_0} = \frac{\frac{Q_1-Q_0}{\overline{Q}}}{\frac{P_1-P_0}{\overline{P}}} = \quad E_{Q_x,P_y} = \frac{\%\Delta Q_x^d}{\%\Delta P_y}.$$

A positive (negative) cross price elasticity indicates that goods X and Y are substitutes (complements).

11.   Suppose a firm's revenues are derived from the sales of two products, X and Y. We may express the firm's revenues as $R = R_X + R_Y$, where $R_X = P_X Q_X$ denotes revenues from the sale of product X, and $R_Y = P_Y Q_Y$ represents the revenue from product Y. The impact of a given percentage change in the price of product X on the total revenues of the firm are given by the following formula:

$$\Delta R = \left[R_X \left(1 + E_{Q_X,P_X} \right) + R_Y E_{Q_Y,P_X} \right] \times \%\Delta P_X.$$

12.   The income elasticity of demand is defined as

$$E_{Q_x,M} = \frac{\%\Delta Q_x^d}{\%\Delta M}.$$

$\angle 0 \rightarrow inf$
$\rangle 0 \rightarrow normal$

A positive (negative) income elasticity indicates that good X is a normal (inferior) good.

13.   For the linear demand function

$$Q_x^d = \alpha_o + \alpha_x P_x + \alpha_y P_y + \alpha_M M + \alpha_H H.$$

$$E = \frac{1}{Slope} \frac{P}{Q}$$

The own price elasticity of demand for good X is given by

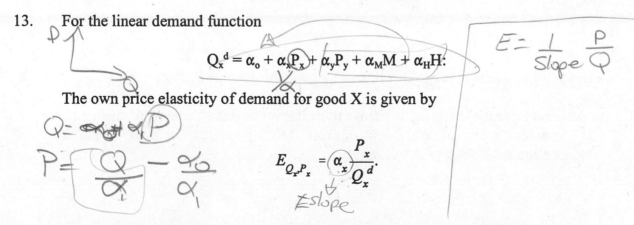

$$E_{Q_x,P_x} = \alpha_x \frac{P_x}{Q_x^d}.$$

Eslope

The cross price elasticity of demand between goods X and Y is given by

41

$$E_{Q_x, P_y} = \alpha_y \frac{P_y}{Q_x^d}.$$

The income elasticity of demand for good X is

$$E_{Q_x, M} = \alpha_M \frac{M}{Q_x^d}.$$

14. For the log-linear demand function:

$$\log Q_x^d = \beta_0 + \beta_x \log P_x + \beta_y \log P_y + \beta_M \log M + \beta_H \log H:$$

The own price elasticity of good X is β_x .

The cross price elasticity of demand between goods X and Y is β_y.

The income elasticity of demand for good X is β_M.

The elasticity of demand of variable H (which might be advertising or some other variable) is β_H.

15. Suppose data that shows when the price of some good is P_1, consumers purchased Q_1 units of the good, and when the price changed to P_2, Q_2 units were purchased. Other things equal, these data can be used to approximate the own price elasticity of demand for the good by using the arc elasticity formula:

$$E_{Q_x, P_x}^{Arc} = \frac{\Delta Q_x^d}{\Delta P_x} \times \frac{Average\ P}{Average\ Q}.$$

In the formula, the average Q is $(Q_1 + Q_2)/2$ and the average P is $(P_1 + P_2)/2$.

16. Marginal Revenue (MR) is the change in total revenue due to a one unit change in output. If E denotes the own price elasticity of demand for a good, the marginal revenue is related to price and the elasticity as follows:

$$MR = P \left[\frac{1 + E}{E} \right].$$

17. Econometrics is the statistical analysis of economic phenomena. Spreadsheet programs such as Excel or Lotus contain programs that allow managers to perform simple econometric techniques, including regression analysis.

18. Suppose the true relationship between two variables, Y and X, is given by

$$Y = a + bX + e,$$

where e is a random variable that has a zero mean. Given data on Y and X, the least squares regression line is the best fit in the sense that it minimizes the sum of squared deviations between the actual data and the line. The least squared parameter estimates (the estimates of the unknown coefficients a and b) are denoted $\hat{a}$ and $\hat{b}$.

19. The *standard error* of each estimated coefficient is a measure of how much each estimated coefficient would vary in regressions based on the same underlying true demand relation, but with different observations. The smaller the standard error of an estimated coefficient, the smaller would be the variation in the estimate given different data.

20. The least squares parameter estimates are unbiased estimators of the true demand parameters whenever the errors (the e_i's) in the true demand relation have a zero mean.

21. When the e_i's are independently and identically distributed normal random variables (in short, *iid normal* random variables), the reported standard errors of the estimated coefficients can be used to perform significance tests.

22. Confidence intervals and t-statistics are used to evaluate the statistical significance of estimated coefficients.

23. If the parameter estimates of a regression equation are $\hat{a}$ and $\hat{b}$, the 95 percent confidence intervals for the true values of a and b can be approximated by

$$\hat{a} \pm 2\sigma_{\hat{a}}$$

and

$$\hat{b} \pm 2\sigma_{\hat{b}}$$

where $\sigma_{\hat{a}}$ and $\sigma_{\hat{b}}$ are the standard errors of $\hat{a}$ and $\hat{b}$ respectively.

43

24. The t-statistic of a parameter estimate is the ratio of the value of the parameter estimate to its standard error. For example, if the parameter estimates are $\hat{a}$ and $\hat{b}$, and the corresponding standard errors are $\sigma_{\hat{a}}$ and $\sigma_{\hat{b}}$, the t-statistic for $\hat{a}$ is

$$t_{\hat{a}} = \frac{\hat{a}}{\sigma_{\hat{a}}}$$

and the t-statistic for $\hat{b}$ is

$$t_{\hat{b}} = \frac{\hat{b}}{\sigma_{\hat{b}}}.$$

25. When the absolute value of the t-statistic is greater than two, the manager can be 95 percent confident that the true value of the underlying parameter in a regression is not zero.

26. Most regression packages report P-values, which are a precise measure of statistical significance. The lower the P-value for an estimated coefficient, the more confident you are in the estimate. Usually, P-values of .05 or below are considered low enough for a researcher to be confident that the estimated coefficient is statistically significant. If the P-value is .05, we say that the estimated coefficient is statistically significant at the 5 percent level.

27. The R-square and the F statistic are two yardsticks frequently used to measure the overall fit of the regression line.

28. The R-Square (also called the coefficient of determination) tells the fraction of the total variation in the dependent variable that is explained by the regression.

29. The value of an R-square ranges from 0 and 1:

$$0 \le R^2 \le 1.$$

The closer the R-square is to 1, the "better" the overall fit of the estimated regression equation to the actual data. Unfortunately, there is no simple cut-off that can be used to determine whether an R-square is close enough to one to indicate a "good" fit.

30. The adjusted R-square is given by

$$\overline{R^2} = 1 - (1 - R^2)\frac{(n - 1)}{(n - k)}$$

44

where n is the total number of observations and k is the number of estimated coefficients. The adjusted R-square "penalizes" the researcher for estimating numerous coefficients from relatively few observations.

31. In performing a regression, the number of parameters to be estimated cannot exceed the number of observations. The difference, n - k, represents the *residual degrees of freedom* after conducting the regression.

32. The main drawback of using the R-square or the adjusted R-square as a gauge of the overall fit of a regression is that no universal rule exists for determining how "high" it must be to indicate a good fit. An alternative measure of goodness of fit, called the *F statistic*, does not suffer from this shortcoming.

33. The F statistic provides a measure of the total variation explained by the regression relative to the total unexplained variation. The greater the F statistic, the better the overall fit of the regression line through the actual data.

34. Regression techniques can also be used to estimate nonlinear relationships among variables. To estimate a log-linear demand function, for instance, the econometrician simply takes the logarithm of prices and quantities before executing the regression routine that minimizes the sum of squared errors.

35. Regression techniques can also be used to perform multiple regressions -- regressions of a dependent variable on multiple explanatory variables.

Questions: Chapter 3

1. Do elasticity and slope mean the same thing? Explain.

No

2. List three factors that affect the magnitude of the own price elasticity of demand, and explain how they affect the elasticity.

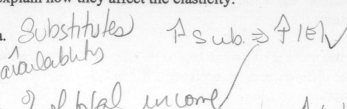

a. Substitutes availability   ↑ sub. ⇒ ↑ |E|

b. % of total income   ↑ % total M ⇒ ↑ |E|

c. time frame |E_{LR}| > |E_{SR}|

3. Use Exhibit 3-1 to graph a linear demand curve. Then answer the accompanying questions.

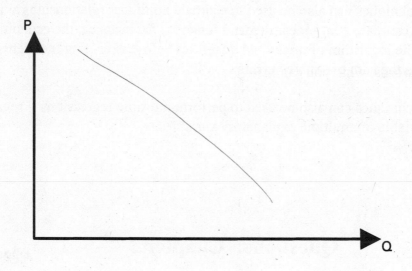

Exhibit 3-1

a. The slope (is, is not) constant along a linear demand curve.
b. The own price elasticity of demand (is, is not) constant along a linear demand curve.
c. As one moves down a linear demand curve, demand becomes (more, less) elastic.

4. Use Exhibit 3-2 to graph a log-linear demand curve. Then answer the accompanying questions.

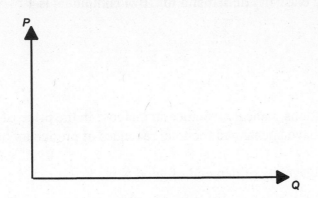

Exhibit 3-2

a. The slope (is, is ~~not~~) constant along a log-linear demand curve.

b. The own price elasticity of demand (is, is not) constant along a log-linear demand curve.

5. Explain, in words, what you can infer about the following situations:

a. The own-price elasticity of demand for Pepsi is -2. $\frac{\%Q}{\%P}$

~~a 10% ↓Δ in P leads to a 20% Δ in Quantity Demanded~~ ✓

b. The cross price elasticity of demand between bread and crackers is 4.

$\frac{\%Q↑}{\%P↑}$ so a 10% drop P bread ⇒ 40% ↑ D cracker ⟹ substitute

$\frac{↑\%Q}{↓\%P}$ <0 complmt $\frac{↓\%Q}{↑\%P}$

c. The cross price elasticity of demand between typewriters and computers is -3.

↑10% ↑ in Pty ⇒ ↓ 30% complmnt

d. The income elasticity of demand for paper is 0.5. $\frac{\%Q}{\%M}$

↑10% mean ⇒ ↑5% paper

normal

e. The income elasticity of demand for whiskey is -1.5. $\frac{\%Q}{\%M}$

↑10% I ⇒ ↓15% m

47

~~Satisfier~~

f.   The advertising elasticity of demand for IBM computers is 1.

No A ⇒ DB ce

6.   For the following situations, indicate whether an increase in the price of good X would increase, decrease, or leave unchanged the total revenues of producers of good X:

P↑

a.   The own price elasticity of demand of good X is -3.

↓ TR

b.   The own price elasticity of demand for good X is -1.

Max @ (E)=-1   ΔP does not affect TR

c.   The own price elasticity of demand for good X is -0.5.

↑TR ✓

✗ 7.   What is a least squares regression?

8.   Suppose an econometrician estimates a log-linear demand function and finds that the estimated coefficient of log P is -2.0. The standard error of the parameter estimate is 0.1, the R-Square is .62, and the F-statistic has a p-value of .005.

a.   Compute the t-statistic for the elasticity of demand.

b.   Is the estimated elasticity significant at the 95 percent level? Explain.

c.   How confident should the researcher be in the overall fit of the regression?
Explain.

Technical Problems: Chapter 3

1.   The demand for company X's product is given by

$$Q_x^d = 10 - 2P_x - 4P_y + 2M.$$

[handwritten: $P_x = 1$ $M=10$ $P_y = 2$]

[handwritten: $Q^d = 10 - 2 - 8 + 20 = 20$]

Good X sells for $1 per unit, good Y sells for $2 per unit, and consumer income is $10.

a.   Calculate the own price elasticity of demand, and state whether demand is elastic, inelastic, or unitary elastic.

[handwritten: $\alpha \frac{P}{Q}$; $-2\left(\frac{1}{20}\right) = -\frac{1}{10} = .01$ inelastic; $\frac{\partial Q}{\partial P} = \frac{\alpha}{2}$; $P = \frac{1}{2}$; $\frac{\alpha}{\partial Q}\frac{P}{Q}$]

b.   Calculate the cross price elasticity of demand between goods X and Y, and determine state whether X and Y are substitutes or complements.

[handwritten: $\alpha_y\left(\frac{P}{Q}\right)$; $-4\left(\frac{2}{20}\right) = -\frac{8}{20} = -\frac{4}{10} = -\frac{2}{5} = -.4$ complements; $\frac{\partial Q}{\partial P_y}$]

49

[handwritten: c) income $\alpha_m\left(\frac{M}{Q}\right) \cdot \frac{2 \times 10}{20} = 1$ > 0 norne]

c. Calculate the income elasticity of demand, and state whether good X is a normal or an inferior good.

2. Suppose the demand for good X has been estimated to be

$$\log Q_x^d = 10 - 3 \log P_x - 2 \log P_y - 4 \log M.$$

a. How can you tell that demand is downward sloping?

b. What is the own price elasticity of demand for good X?

c. What is the cross price elasticity of demand between goods X and Y?

d. Are goods X and Y substitutes or complements?

e. What is the income elasticity of demand for good X?

f. Is good X a normal or an inferior good?

g. If income increased by 5 percent, what would happen to the demand for good X?

h. If the price of good Y decreased by 1 percent, what would happen to the demand for good X?

i.   If the price of good X increased by 2 percent, what would happen to the quantity demanded of good X?

j.   If producers of good X increased their prices, what would happen to their revenues?

3.   Your research department has estimated the own price elasticity of demand for movie tickets to be -2. If the price of movies increased by 10 percent, what would happen to the quantity of tickets sold and the ticket revenues of your firm? $\frac{\%Q}{\%P} = -2$

4.   Your research department has estimated the advertising elasticity of demand for your product to be -1.94. Your boss is concerned about declining profits and revenues, and wants to increase your firm's level of advertising by 10 percent. Would this be advisable? Explain.

$$\frac{\%Q}{\%A} = -1.94$$

↑ %A 10% ⇒ ↓ Q^D by 19.4%

no adv   1) reduce ad

5.   An econometrician hired by your firm estimates the demand relation

$$P = a + bQ + e$$

and finds $\hat{a} = 10$; $\hat{b} = -2$; $\sigma_{\hat{a}} = 10$; $\sigma_{\hat{b}} = 20$.

a.   Find the 95 percent confidence interval for the true values of a and b.

b.   What are the values of the t-statistics for the parameter estimates?

c.   Would it be advisable to use this estimated demand equation to help you make managerial decisions? Explain.

6.   An econometrician hired by your firm estimated the following relation between your firm's sales (S) and advertising (A):

$$\log S = a + b \log A + e$$

and finds $\hat{a} = 100$; $\hat{b} = 1.52$; $\sigma_{\hat{a}} = 10$; $\sigma_{\hat{b}} = 0.20$. In addition, the R-square is .82 and the F-statisic is significant at a level of 0.5.

a.   How much would your firm's sales change if you increased advertising by 10 percent?

b.   Can you be 95 percent confident that an increase in advertising would increase your firm's sales? Explain.

c.   Overall, how much confidence to you place in the analysis conducted by the consultant? Why?

7. Fiberboard, Inc. hired a consultant to estimate the demand for its cardboard boxes. The consultant collected data on the price and quantity of boxes sold, as well as data on customer incomes and advertising outlays. The consultant computed the logarithm of each variable and then used Excel to estimate a log-linear demand function. The results of the regression are:

Regression Statistics

Multiple R	0.92
R Square	0.84
Adjusted R Square	0.80
Standard Error	42.07
Observations	15.00

Analysis of Variance

	df	Sum of Squares	Mean Square	F	Significance F
Regression	3.00	103270.80	34423.60	19.45	0.00
Residual	11.00	19472.62	1770.24		
Total	14.00	122743.42			

	Coefficients	Standard Error	t Statistic	P-value	Lower 95%	Upper 95%
Intercept	89.93	35.06	2.57	0.02	12.77	167.09
Log (Price)	-2.44	0.42	-5.84	0.00	-3.36	-1.52
Log(Income)	1.54	0.44	3.51	0.00	0.58	2.51
Log(Advertising)	0.27	0.16	1.74	0.10	-0.07	0.62

a. Based on these estimates, what is the demand function for Fiberboard's cardboard boxes?

b. Management is considering raising the price of its boxes. Based on the estimated demand equation, what would be the expected impact of a 10 percent price increase on the number of boxes sold?

c. If the firm raises price by 10 percent, will the firm's revenues rise or fall?

8.   You are the owner of a bookstore, earn revenues primarily from selling coffee and books. For the past two years you have consistently earned, on average, revenues of $500 per week from selling coffee and $1,000 per week from selling books. If the own-price elasticity of demand for coffee is –1.0 and the cross-price elasticity of demand between books and coffee is –1.8, what would happen to your revenues if you lowered the price of coffee by 10 percent?

Multiple Choice and True/False Questions: Chapter 3

1.   If the demand for a product is log Q_x^d = 10 - 5 log P_x , product X is
      a. Elastic
      b. Inelastic
      c. Unitary elastic
      d. Cannot be determined without more information.

2.   If the quantity demanded of beer falls by 10% when price increases 10% we know that the own-price elasticity of beer is:
      a. - 10
      b. 10
      c. -1/2
      d. -1

3.   If demand is perfectly elastic, the absolute value of the own price elasticity of demand is:
      a. 0
      b. 1
      c. infinity
      d. none of the above.

4.   Demand is more elastic in the long-term because consumers:
        a.   are patient
        b.   have more time to seek out available substitutes
        c.   they spend a larger share of their budget in the short-term
        d.   none of the above

5.   If the cross-price elasticity between ketchup and mustard is 4, a 10% increase in the price
        of mustard will lead to a:
        a.   40% drop in the quantity demanded of ketchup
        b.   40% drop in the quantity demanded of mustard
        c.   40% increase in the quantity demanded of ketchup
        d.   40% increase in the quantity demanded of mustard

6.   A positive income elasticity tells us that the good is:
        a.   a normal good
        b.   a substitute good
        c.   an inferior good
        d.   an inelastic good

7.   A person who performs the statistical analysis of economic phenomenon is known as:
        a.   an econometrician
        b.   an economist
        c.   a statistical economist
        d.   an econometric statistician

8.   As a rule of thumb, a parameter estimate is not statistically different from zero when the
        absolute value of the t-statistic is:
        a.   greater than 2
        b.   less than 2
        c.   greater than the variance
        d.   greater than the square root of the parameter estimate

9.   The elasticity of variable G with respect to variable S measures
        a.   the slope of G
        b.   the slope of S
        c.   the percentage change in G that will result from a given percentage change in S
        d.   the change in variable G that results from a given change in variable S

10.   When the own price elasticity of demand is -1:
        a.   demand is inelastic
        b.   total revenue falls when the price of good X rises
        c.   total revenue rises when the price of good X rises
        d.   none of the above

11. The demand for violins has been estimated to be:

$$Q_v = 145 - 100P_v + 20\,M$$

Based on the estimated demand equation we can conclude:
a. violins are inferior goods.
b. the demand for violins is elastic.
c. the demand for violins is inelastic.
d. none of the above.

12. True or False: If demand is perfectly inelastic, then the own price elasticity of demand is infinite in absolute value.

13. True or False: If demand is perfectly elastic, a small increase in price will lead to a situation where none of the good is purchased.

14. True or False: The elasticity of demand is constant along a linear demand curve.

15. True or False: The demand for drinks is more elastic than the demand for Pepsi.

16. True or False: If the p-value for an estimated coefficient is 0.01, then the estimated coefficient is statistically significant at the 1 percent level.

17. True or False: If a firm decreases the price of its product, its total revenue will decrease.

18. True or False: As the price of X falls and we move down a linear demand curve for X, demand becomes more elastic.

19. True or False: When the price of gum was "low", consumers in the U.S. spent a total of $2 billion annually on gum consumption. When the price doubled, consumer expenditures actually increased to $3 billion annually. This indicates that the demand for gum is upward sloping.

20. True or False: The F-statistic provides a guage of the overall fit of a regression equation that is preferable to the R-square because the statistical properties of the F-statistic are known.

Answers to Questions: Chapter 3

1. No. An elasticity measures the impact of a percentage change in one variable on the percentage change in another. A slope measures the impact of a change in one variable on the value of another. Since an elasticity compares percentage changes, it is not sensitive to the units in which the variables are measured. This is not the case for the slope.

2. a. Available substitutes. The more available substitutes, the more elastic the demand.

   b. Time. The greater the time to seek out substitutes, the more elastic the demand. Thus, demand tends to be more inelastic in the short run than in the long run.

   c. Expenditure share. The greater the share of one's budget allocated to a good, the more elastic is its demand.

3. A linear demand curve is shown in Exhibit 3-3.

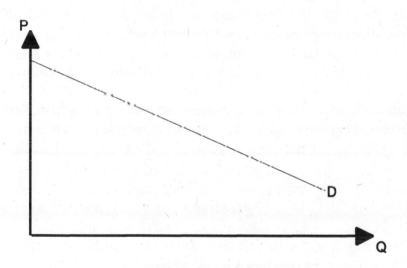

Exhibit 3-3

   a. is

   b. is not

   c. less

4.   A log-linear demand curve is shown in Exhibit 3-4.

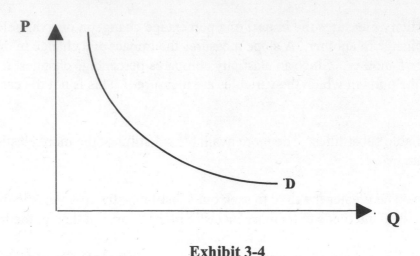

Exhibit 3-4

a.   is not

b.   is

5.   a.   Since the own price elasticity of demand for Pepsi is -2, we know demand is
         elastic (it is greater than one in absolute value). Furthermore, a 10 percent
         increase in the price of Pepsi will reduce the quantity demanded by 20 percent.

      b.   Since the cross price elasticity of demand between bread and crackers is 4, we
         know bread and crackers are substitutes (the cross price elasticity is positive). A
         10 percent increase in the price of crackers will increase the demand for bread by
         40 percent.

      c.   Since the cross price elasticity of demand between typewriters and computers is
         given as -3, we know typewriters and computers are complements (the cross price
         elasticity is negative). A 10 percent increase in the price of typewriters will
         reduce the demand for computers by 30 percent.

      d.   Since the income elasticity of demand for paper is 0.5, we know paper is a normal
         good (the income elasticity is positive). A 10 percent increase in income will
         increase the demand for paper by 5 percent.

      e.   Since the income elasticity of demand for whiskey is -1.5, we know whiskey is an
         inferior good (the income elasticity is negative). A 10 percent increase in income
         will reduce the demand for whiskey by 15 percent.

f.   Since the advertising elasticity of demand for IBM computers is 1, we know advertising increases the demand for IBM computers (the advertising elasticity is positive). A 10 percent increase in advertising will increase the demand for IBM computers by 10 percent.

6.   a.   Demand is elastic (the absolute value of the elasticity exceeds 1), so an increase in price would decrease total revenues.

       b.   Demand is unitary elastic (the elasticity is 1 in absolute value), so an increase in price would not affect total revenues.

       c.   Demand is inelastic (the absolute value of the elasticity is less than 1), so an increase in price would increase total revenues.

7.   A least squares regression is a statistical technique used to estimate things like demand equations. It is the line that minimizes the sum of squared errors between the actual observations and the line through the points.

8.   a. $t = -2.0/0.1 = -20$.

       b.   Since $|t| = 20 > 2$, the parameter estimate is statistically significant at the 95 percent level.

       c.   Very confident. The p-value of .005 suggests that their is only 5 chances out of 1000 that the regression fit the data due purely to chance.

Answers to Technical Problems: Chapter 3

1.   a.   -0.1, inelastic. Notice that at the given prices and income, $Q_x^d = 20$. Using the formula for the own price elasticity of demand for linear demand, the own price elasticity is $-2(1)/(20) = -0.1$. Since this is less than one in absolute value, the demand for X is inelastic.

       b.   -0.4, complements. Notice that at the given prices and income, $Q_x^d = 20$. Using the formula for the cross price elasticity of demand for linear demand, the cross price elasticity is $-4(2)/(20) = -0.4$. Since this is negative, X and Y are complements.

c. 1, normal. Notice that at the given prices and income, $Q_x^d = 20$. Using the formula for the income elasticity of demand for linear demand, the income elasticity is $+2(10)/(20) = 1$. Since this is positive, X is a normal good.

2.
a. Because the coefficient of log P_x is negative.

b. -3. Since this is a log-linear demand function, the coefficient of log P_x is the own price elasticity of good X.

c. -2. Since this is a log-linear demand function, the coefficient of log P_y is the cross price elasticity between goods X and Y.

d. Complements, since the cross price elasticity is negative.

e. -4. Since this is a log-linear demand function, the coefficient of log M is the income elasticity of demand for good X.

f. Inferior, since the income elasticity is negative.

g. Decrease by 20 percent. To see this, use the general formula for the income elasticity of demand to write $-4 = \%\Delta Q_x^d/.05$. Solving give us $\%\Delta Q_x^d = -0.2$, or a decrease of 20 percent.

h. Increase by 2 percent. To see this, use the general formula for the cross price elasticity of demand to write $-2 = \%\Delta Q_x^d/(-.01)$. Solving give us $\%\Delta Q_x^d = 0.02$, or an increase of 2 percent.

i. Decrease by 6 percent. To see this, use the general formula for the own price elasticity of demand to write $-3 = \%\Delta Q_x^d/.02$. Solving give us $\%\Delta Q_x^d = -0.06$, or a decrease of 6 percent.

j. Revenues would fall, since demand is elastic (the own price elasticity of demand is greater than one in absolute value).

3. Quantity demanded would fall by 20 percent. Total revenue would fall, since demand is elastic.

4. Since the advertising elasticity is negative, an increase in advertising would actually decrease the demand for your firm's product. Thus, it is not advisable to increase advertising. In fact, by increasing advertising by 10 percent, your firm's demand would fall by 19.4 percent.

5.   a.   The 95 percent confidence interval for the true value of a is

$$\hat{a} \pm 2\sigma_{\hat{a}}$$

which is 10 - 2(10) = -10 and 10 + 2(10) = 30. Thus you can be 95 percent confident that the true value of a lies between -10 and 30. Similarly, the 95 percent confidence interval for b is -2 - 2(20) = -42 and -2 + 2(20) = 38. Thus you can be 95 percent confident that the true value of b lies between -42 and 38.

b.   The t-statistics are the ratio of the parameter estimate to its standard error. Thus, the t-statistic for the estimate of a is 10/10 = 1. The t-statistic for the estimate for b is -2/20 = -0.1.

c.   No. The confidence intervals are not very tight, and in fact you can't even be 95 percent confident that the demand curve slopes downward. The t-statistics are considerably less than one in absolute value, indicating the parameter estimates are not very precise.

6.   a.   The parameter b represents the elasticity of sales (S) with respect to advertising (A). Since the advertising elasticity of sales is estimated to be 1.52, we know that a 10 percent increase in advertising will lead to a 15.2 percent increase in sales.

b.   Yes, because the lower bound on the 95 percent confidence interval for b is given by 1.52 - 2(0.20) = 1.12, which is greater than zero.

c.   Not very much. The p-value for the F-statistic suggests a very poor overall fit. In fact, the value of 0.5 means that you would expect the estimated relation between sales and advertising to arise purely out of chance. The fact that the regression does not include income or prices as explanatory varibles might account for this deficiency.

7.   a. $\log Q_x^d = 89.93 - 2.44 \log P_x + 1.54 \log M + 0.27 \log A$

b.   Since this is a log-linear demand, the own-price elasticity of demand is -2.44. Using the elasticity formula, $-2.44 = \%\Delta Q_x^d / \%\Delta P_x = \%\Delta Q_x^d / 10\%$. Solving for the percentage change in quantity demanded reveals that quantity demanded decreases by 24.4%.

c.   Demand is elastic. By the total revenue test, the increase in price leads to a decrease in the firm's revenues.

8.   We can use the formula $\Delta R = \left[R_X \left(1 + E_{Q_X, P_X} \right) + R_Y E_{Q_Y, P_X} \right] \times \% \Delta P_X$ by letting X denote coffee sales, Y denote book sales, $R_X = \$500$ denote coffee revenues, $R_Y = \$1,000$ denote book revenues, $E_{Q_X, P_X} = -1.0$ denote the own-price elasticity of demand for coffee, $E_{Q_Y, P_X} = -1.8$ denote the cross-price elasticity of demand between coffee and books, and noting that the proposed change in the price of coffee is $\% \Delta P_x = -10\%$. Plugging these numbers into the above formula reveals

$$\Delta R = \left[\$500 \left(1 - 1 \right) + \$1,000 \left(-1.8 \right) \right] \times \left(-10\% \right)$$
$$= \$0 + \$180$$
$$= \$180 \, .$$

In other words, lowering the price of coffee by 10 percent does not affect coffee revenues (since demand is unitary elastic) but increases book revenues by $180.

Answers to Multiple Choice and True/False Questions: Chapter 3

1.   a
2.   d
3.   c
4.   b
5.   c
6.   a
7.   a
8.   b
9.   c
10.   d
11.   d
12.   False; it's zero
13.   True
14.   False
15.   False; more inelastic
16.   True
17.   False; only if demand is inelastic
18.   False; more inelastic
19.   False; demand is inelastic
20.   True

Chapter 4
The Theory of Individual Behavior

Chapter 4 at a Glance

Key Concepts: Chapter 4

1.   Consumer opportunities represent the possible goods and services consumers can afford to consume, while consumer preferences determine which of these goods will be consumed.

2.   If the consumer views bundles A and B to be equally satisfying, we say she is indifferent between bundles A and B. A ~ B is the shorthand notation used to represent indifference.

3.   If the consumer view bundle A to be better than bundle B, we say she prefers bundle A to bundle B. A ≻ B is the shorthand notation used to represent the fact that if given a choice between bundle A and bundle B the consumer would choose bundle A.

4.   An indifference curve defines the combinations of goods X and Y that give the consumer the same level of satisfaction. That is, the consumer is indifferent between any combination of goods along an indifference curve.

5.   The absolute value of the slope of an indifference curve is called the Marginal Rate of Substitution (MRS). The marginal rate of substitution between two goods is the rate at which a consumer can substitute one good for another and still maintain the same level of satisfaction.

6.   The consumer's preference ordering is assumed to satisfy four basic properties: completeness, more is better, diminishing marginal rate of substitution, and transitivity.

   a.   Completeness insures that the consumer is capable of expressing a preference for (or indifference between) all bundles.

   b.   More is better means that if bundle A has at least as much of every good as bundle B, and strictly more of some good, then the consumer strictly prefers bundle A to bundle B.

   c.   Diminishing marginal rate of substitution means that as a consumer obtains more of good X, the rate at which she is willing to substitute good X for Y decreases. This implies that indifference curves are convex from the origin.

   d.   Transitivity means that, for any three bundles A, B, and C, if A ≻ B and B ≻ C, then A ≻ C. Similarly, if A ~ B and B ~ C, then A ~ C.

7.   The opportunity set (also called the budget set) defines the set of consumption bundles that are affordable, given income (M), the price of good X (P_x), and the price of good Y (P_y). It is may be expressed mathematically as

$$P_xX + P_yY \leq M.$$

8.   The budget line defines the combination of consumption bundles that fully exhausts the consumer's budget:

$$P_xX + P_yY = M.$$

9.   The slope of the budget line is given by $-P_x/P_y$, and represents the market rate of substitution between goods X and Y.

10.   An increase in income leads to a parallel, outward shift in the budget line.

11.   An increase in the price of good X rotates the budget line clockwise.

12.   The equilibrium consumption bundle is the affordable bundle that yields the greatest satisfaction to the consumer.

13.   When prices or income change, the equilibrium consumption bundle of a utility maximizing consumer will change.

14.   Goods X and Y are called substitutes if an increase (a decrease) in the price of good X leads to an increase (a decrease) in the consumption of good Y.

15.   Goods X and Y are called complements if an increase (a decrease) in the price of good X leads to a decrease (an increase) in the consumption of good Y.

16.   Good X is a normal good if an increase (a decrease) in income leads to an increase (a decrease) in the consumption of good X.

17.   Good X is an inferior good if an increase (a decrease) in income leads to a decrease (an increase) in the consumption of good X.

18.   The effect of a price increase on demand is composed of substitution and income effects. The substitution effect reflects a movement along an indifference curve, thus isolating the effect of a relative price change on consumption. The income effect results from a parallel shift in the budget line, and thus isolates the effect of a change in "real income" on consumption.

19. An individual's demand curve for good X indicates the amount of good X a utility maximizing consumer will purchase at various prices of good X, taking as given prices of other goods and income.

20. The market demand curve is the horizontal summation of individual demand curves, and indicates the total quantity all consumers in the market would purchase at each price.

Questions: Chapter 4

1. In each of the following situations, explain which property of preferences, if any, is violated.

   a. Sam prefers one pound of beef to one pound of chicken, and one pound of chicken to two pounds of chicken.

   b. Sam prefers one pound of beef to one pound of chicken, and one pound of chicken to two pounds of pork.

   c. Sam's indifference curve is such that he is willing to give up one pound of beef in order to receive his first pound of chicken, and will give up two more pounds of beef to get a second pound of chicken.

      dimin MRS

   d. Sam doesn't know whether he prefers one pound of chicken or one pound of beef.

      complet

   e. Sam doesn't care whether he gets one pound of beef or one pound of chicken.

   f. Sam prefers one pound of beef to a pound of chicken, a pound of chicken to two pounds of pork, and two pounds of pork to one pound of beef.

      1B>1C
      1C>2P
      2P>1B   *non completeness*

2. Suppose the price of good X is $3, the price of good Y is $5, and the consumer's income is $30.

   a. What is the equation for the budget line?

      $3x + 5y = 30$

b.	Write the budget line in slope-intercept form.

$$y = \frac{30}{5} - \frac{3x}{5} = 6 - \frac{3}{5}x$$

c.	What is the maximum amount of good X that can be purchased?

$$x = 10$$

d.	What is the maximum amount of good Y that can be purchased?

$$y = 6$$

e.	What is the slope of the budget line.

$$-\frac{3}{5}$$

f.	Graph the budget line in Exhibit 4-1.

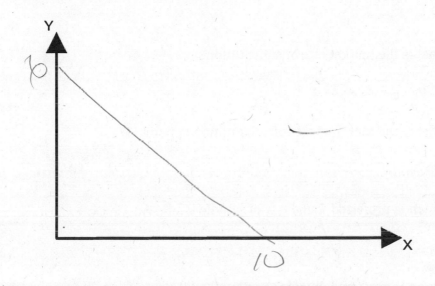

Exhibit 4-1

3.	Exhibit 4-2 shows the budget constraint and indifference curves for a consumer with an income of $100. Based on this information, answer the following questions:

a.	What is the price of good Y?

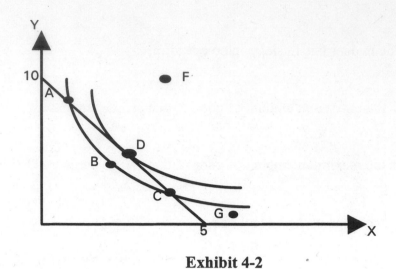

Exhibit 4-2

$M = 100$

$P_x = 20$

b.   What is the price of good X?

$P_y = 10$

$20x + 10y = 100$

$y = \dfrac{100}{10} - \dfrac{20}{10}x$

c.   What is the market rate of substitution?

$+2$

d.   What is the marginal rate of substitution at point D?

2

e.   Which is preferred, bundle A or bundle B?

$Ind.$

f.   Which is preferred, bundle D or bundle F?

F

g.   Which is preferred, bundle G or bundle B?

B

h.   Is bundle F affordable?

N

i.   What point represents consumer equilibrium?

D

68

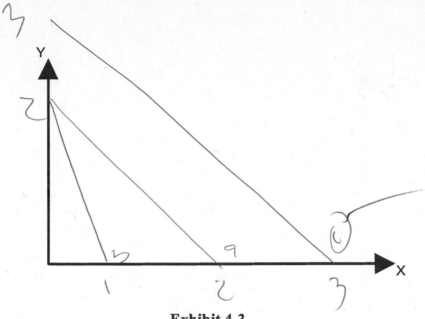

Exhibit 4-3

$$5x + 5y = 10$$

4.   Use Exhibit 4-3 to answer these questions:

   a.   Suppose the price of good X is $5, the price of good Y is $5, and a consumer has $10 in income. Graph the budget line.

   b.   Now suppose the price of good X rises to $10, but the price of good Y remains at $5 and income remains at $10. Graph the new budget line. $10x + 5y = 10$

   c.   Graph the budget line when the price of good X remains at $5, the price of good Y remains at $5, but income rises to $15. $5x + 5y = 15$

5.   Suppose goods X and Y are substitutes. Use Exhibit 4-4 to show how consumer equilibrium changes if the price of good X falls.

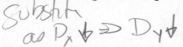

Substh
as $P_x \downarrow \Rightarrow D_y \downarrow$

Exhibit 4-4

6. Suppose good X is a normal good but good Y is an inferior good. Use Exhibit 4-5 to show how equilibrium changes if income increases.

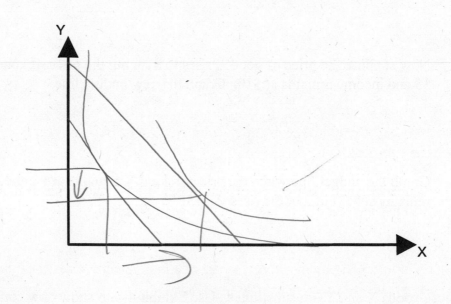

Exhibit 4-5

70

Technical Problems: Chapter 4

1. Mitchell has $10 in income, and can use this at the ACME Candy store to buy either jellybeans or chocolate. Jellybeans cost $1 per pound, but chocolate costs $5 per pound. Mitchell maximizes utility by purchasing 5 pounds of jellybeans and 1 pound of chocolate. Illustrate consumer equilibrium in Exhibit 4-6.

$$1_j + 5c = 10$$
$$5_j + 1c - 10$$

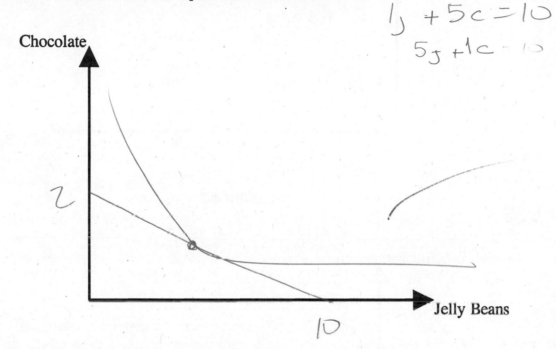

Exhibit 4-6

2. Suppose ACME Candy (in problem 1) offers Mitchell a buy one pound of chocolate, get one pound free deal.

    a. Graph Mitchell's budget constraint in Exhibit 4-7 under this deal, assuming he still has income of $10 and prices are as in problem 1.

    b. Will Mitchell buy more than 5 pounds of jellybeans, given the buy-one, get one free deal? Explain, using Exhibit 4-8.

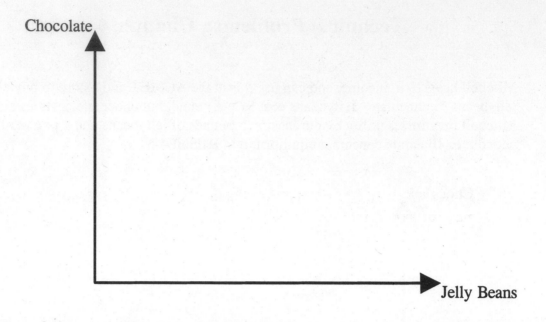

Exhibit 4-7

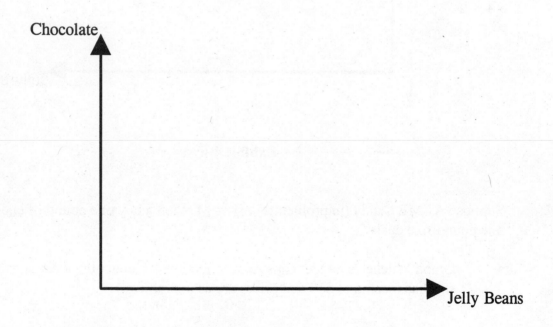

Exhibit 4-8

3. Susie and Joan have very different preferences and income, but both shop at the same grocery store. Last week Joan bought $10 worth of vegetables and $5 worth of meat. Susie bought $5 worth of vegetables and $30 worth of meat. What must be true about Susie's marginal rate of substitution between meat and vegetables compared to Joan's?

4. Joe currently buys 4 units of good X and 3 units of good Y. Use Exhibit 4-9 to show that Joe is made better off if the price of good Y falls.

4→X
3→Y

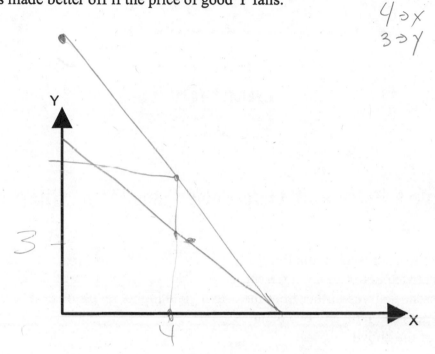

Exhibit 4-9

5. Answer the following questions on the basis of Exhibit 4-10.

    a. Good X is a (normal, inferior) good.

    b. Goods Y is a (normal, inferior) good.

    c. The movement from A to B is called the _____ effect.

    d. The movement from B to C is called the _____ effect.

73

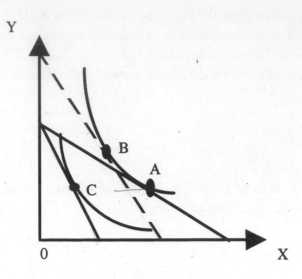

Exhibit 4-10

Multiple Choice and True/False Questions: Chapter 4

1.   The "more is better" axiom implies that
      a.   indifference curves do not intersect.
      b.   indifference curves farther from the origin yield higher levels of satisfaction.
      c.   consumers can rank any two bundles.
      d.   None of the above.

2.   Which of the following is true?
      a.   Indifference curves are generally straight lines.
      b.   At a point of consumer equilibrium, the MRS equals 1.
      c.   If income increases, a consumer will always consume more of at least one good.
      d.   None of the above are true.

3.   A decrease in the price of good X will have what affect on the budget line on a normal X-Y graph?
      a.   parallel outward shift of the line
      b.   increase the vertical intercept
      c.   decrease the horizontal intercept
      d.   none of the above.

4.   If the prices of both X and Y double the consumer would reduce his or her consumption of good X if it is
      a. a normal good.
      b. an inferior good.
      c. a substitute for Y.
      d. a complement for Y.

5.   The slope of the budget line is:
      a. $-P_x/P_y$
      b. M/P_x
      c. M/P_y
      d. $-P_y/P_x$

6.   The notation A ≻ B means
      a. bundle A has more in it than bundle B.
      b. bundle A is preferred to bundle B.
      c. the consumer is indifferent between bundle A and B.
      d. bundle B is preferred to bundle A.

7.   Along the same indifference curve, the MRS is
      a. constant as more of good Y is consumed.
      b. increases as more of good X is consumed.
      c. diminishes as more of good X is consumed.
      d. diminishes as more of good Y is consumed.

8.   Which of the following rules out an endless cycle in the consumer's decision process?
      a. consumer sovereignty.
      b. more and better.
      c. diminishing marginal rate of substitution.
      d. transitivity.

9.   The absolute value of the slope of the indifference curve represents
      a. the marginal rate of substitution.
      b. the market rate of substitution.
      c. the budget rate of substitution.
      d. the opportunity rate of substitution.

10.   When the price of a good falls with other things unchanged, the real income of the consumer
      a. is unchanged.
      b. increases.
      c. decreases.
      d. may rise or fall, depending on whether the good is normal or inferior.

75

11. Consider a two good world, with commodities X and Y. If X is an inferior good, then an increase in consumer income cannot
    a. decrease the demand for Y.
    b. decrease the demand for X.
    c. increase the demand for Y.
    d. make the consumer better off.

12. True or False: If money income doubles and the prices of all goods double, then the consumer is worse off because of the inflation.

13. True or False: Increases in income lead to increases in the consumption of all goods.

14. True or False: The income effect of an increase in the price of good X isolates the effect of a change in relative prices on the consumption of each good.

15. True or False: The greater the price of good X, the greater the MRS of a consumer who is in equilibrium.

16. The "more is better" property of consumer preferences implies that indifference curves cannot be upward sloping.

17. Diminishing marginal rate of substitution means that indifference curves are convex from the origin.

Answers to Questions: Chapter 4

1. a.   more is better.

    b.   no properties are violated; beef, chicken and pork are different commodities, so more is better is not violated.

    c.   diminishing marginal rate of substitution.

    d.   completeness

    e.   no properties are violated; Sam is indifferent between the two bundles.

    f.   transitivity

2. a. $3X + 5Y = 30$

    b. $Y = 6 - (3/5)X.$

    c.   10 units.

    d.   6 units.

    e.   -3/5

    f.   See Exhibit 4-11.

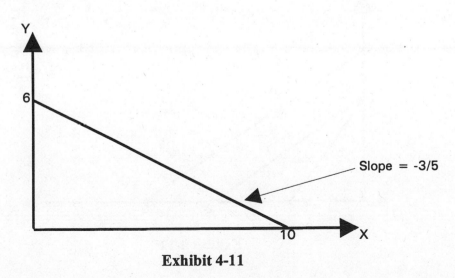

Exhibit 4-11

3.	a.	10, since $\$100/P_y = 10$ implies $P_y = 10$.

	b.	20, since $\$100/P_x = 5$ implies $P_x = 20$.

	c.	2, since $|-P_x/P_y| = |-20/10| = 2$.

	d.	2, since in equilibrium the MRS equals the market rate of substitution.

	e.	Neither; the consumer is indifferent between them.

	f.	F.

	g.	Bundle B. Notice that if an indifference curve were drawn through point G, it would be lower than the one through point B.

	h.	No.

	i.	D

4.	a.	See budget line labeled a in Exhibit 4-12.

	b.	See budget line labeled b in Exhibit 4-12.

	c.	See the budget line labeled c in Exhibit 4-12.

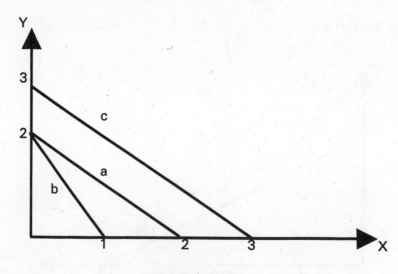

Exhibit 4-12

5.   The budget line rotates from 1 to 2 in Exhibit 4-13 and equilibrium moves from A to B.

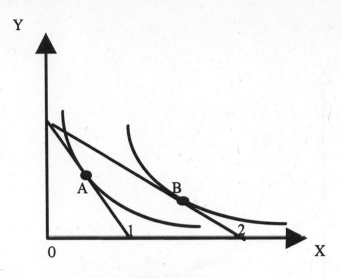

Exhibit 4-13

6.   The budget line shifts parallel from 1 to 2 in Exhibit 4-14 and equilibrium moves from A to B.

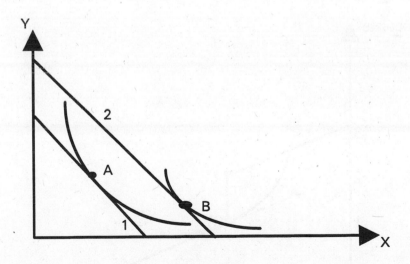

Exhibit 4-14

Answers to Technical Problems: Chapter 4

1. See Exhibit 4-15.

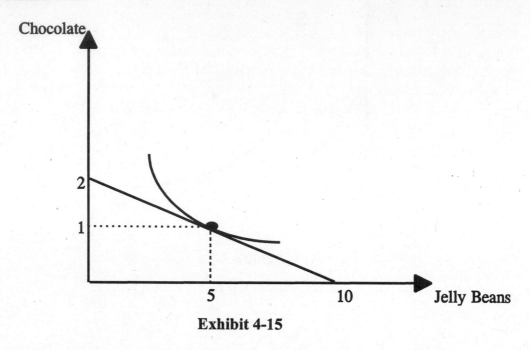

Exhibit 4-15

2. a. The budget line is ABCD in Exhibit 4-16.

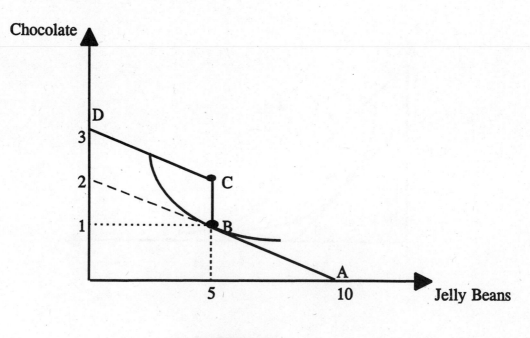

Exhibit 4-16

b.   No. The reason is that, to buy more than 5 pounds of jelly beans, Mitchell would end up on segment AB of his budget constraint, which would yield lower satisfaction. See Exhibit 4-16.

3.   Assuming they both face the same prices, their marginal rates of substitution between meat and vegetables must be equal. This is because, in equilibrium, each will set their MRS equal to the market rate of substitution: $MRS_{Susie} = P_{meat}/P_{veg} = MRS_{Joan}$.

4.   In Exhibit 4-17, I1 > I0, so Joe is better off in moving from A to B.

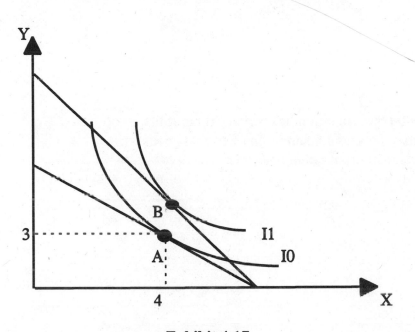

Exhibit 4-17

5.   a.   normal

     b.   normal

     c.   substitution

     d.   income

81

Answers to Multiple Choice and True/False Questions:
Chapter 4

1. b
2. c
3. d
4. a
5. a
6. b
7. c
8. d
9. a
10. b
11. a
12. False; the budget constraint is unchanged, so utility is too
13. False; only increases consumption of normal goods
14. False; the substitution effect does this
15. True
16. True
17. True

Chapter 5
The Production Process and Costs

Chapter 5 at a Glance

Key Concepts: Chapter 5

1.   The production function, denoted

$$Q = F(K, L)$$

is a "recipe" that defines the maximum amount of output that can be produced with K units of capital and L units of labor.

2.   Variable factors of production are the inputs a manager may adjust in order to alter production. Fixed factors are inputs the manager is not able to adjust.

3.   The average product (AP) of an input is defined as total product divided by the quantity used of the input. In particular, the average product of labor is

$$AP_L = \frac{Q}{L},$$

and the average product of capital is

$$AP_K = \frac{Q}{K}.$$

Thus, average product is a measure of the output produced per unit of input.

4.   The marginal product (MP) of an input is defined as the change in total output attributable to the last unit of an input.   The marginal product of capital (MP_K) is therefore the change in total output divided by the change in capital:

$$MP_K = \frac{\Delta Q}{\Delta K}.$$

The marginal product of labor (MP_L) is the change in total output divided by the change in labor:

$$MP_L = \frac{\Delta Q}{\Delta L}.$$

5.   As the usage of an input increases, marginal product initially increases (increasing marginal returns), then begins to decline (decreasing marginal returns), and eventually becomes negative (negative marginal returns).

6. The value marginal product of an input is the value of the output produced by the last unit of an input. If each unit of output can be sold at a price of P, then the value marginal product of labor is:

$$VMP_L = P \times MP_L,$$

and the value marginal product of capital is:

$$VMP_K = P \times MP_K.$$

7. In order to maximize profits, a manager should use inputs at levels where the marginal benefit equals the marginal cost. More specifically, when the price of each additional unit of labor is w, the manager should continue to employ labor up to the point where $VMP_L = w$, in the range of diminishing marginal product.

8. The linear production function is

$$Q = F(K, L) = a\,K + b\,L.$$

9. The Leontief (or fixed-proportions) production function is

$$Q = F(K, L) = \min\{b\,K, c\,L\}.$$

10. The Cobb-Douglas production function is

$$Q = F(K, L) = K^a\,L^b.$$

11. If the production function is linear and given by

$$Q = F(K, L) = a\,K + b\,L,$$

then

$$MP_K = a,$$

and

$$MP_L = b.$$

12. If the production function is Cobb-Douglas and given by

$$Q = F(K, L) = K^a\,L^b,$$

then

$$MP_L = bK^a\,L^{b-1},$$

and

$$MP_K = aK^{a-1}L^b.$$

13. An isoquant defines the combinations of inputs (K and L) that yield the producer the same level of output. That is, any combination of capital and labor along an isoquant produces the same level of output.

14. The marginal rate of technical substitution (MRTS) determines the rate at which a producer can substitute between two inputs while maintaining the same level of output. The $MRTS_{KL}$ is the absolute value of the slope of the isoquant, and is simply the ratio of the marginal products:

$$MRTS_{KL} = \frac{MP_L}{MP_K}.$$

15. The production function satisfies the law of diminishing marginal rate of technical substitution if, as a producer uses less of an input, increasingly more of the other input must be employed in order to produce the same level of output.

16. An isocost line represents the combinations of K and L that cost the firm the same amount of money.

17. For given input prices, isocosts farther from the origin are associated with higher costs. Changes in input prices change the slope of isocost lines.

18. In order to minimize the cost of producing a given level of output, the marginal product per dollar spent should be equal for all inputs:

$$\frac{MP_L}{w} = \frac{MP_K}{r}.$$

Equivalently, to minimize the cost of production a firm should employ inputs such that the marginal rate of technical substitution is equal to the ratio of input prices:

$$\frac{MP_L}{MP_K} = \frac{w}{r}.$$

19. In order to minimize the cost of producing a given level of output, the firm manager should use less of an input when its price rises, and more of other inputs.

20. Fixed costs, denoted FC, are costs that do not vary with output. Fixed costs include the costs of fixed inputs used in production.

21. Variable costs, denoted VC(Q), are costs that change when output is changed. Variable costs include the costs of inputs that vary with output.

22. In the presence of fixed factors of production, the short-run cost function summarizes the minimum possible cost of producing each level of output when variable factors are being used in the cost-minimizing way.

23. Average fixed cost (AFC) is defined as fixed costs (FC) divided by the number of units of output:

$$AFC = \frac{FC}{Q}.$$

24. Average variable cost (AVC) is defined as variable cost (VC) divided by the number of units of output (Q):

$$AVC = \frac{VC(Q)}{Q}.$$

25. Average total cost (ATC) is total cost divided by the number of units of output:

$$ATC = \frac{C(Q)}{Q}.$$

26. Marginal cost (MC) is the change in cost attributable to the last unit of output:

$$MC = \frac{\Delta C}{\Delta Q}.$$

27. Sunk costs are those costs that are forever lost after they have been paid. Sunk costs are irrelevant in decision-making, although they will affect your bottom-line.

28. The cubic cost function is given by $C(Q) = f + aQ + bQ^2 + cQ^3$, where a, b, c, and f are fixed numbers.

29. For a cubic cost function, $C(Q) = f + aQ + bQ^2 + cQ^3$, the marginal cost function is $MC(Q) = a + 2bQ + 3cQ^2$.

30. The long run average cost curve defines the minimum average cost of producing alternative levels of output, allowing for optimal selection of all variables of production (both fixed and variable factors).

31.   Economies of scale exist whenever long run average costs decline as output is increased. Diseconomies of scale exist when long run average costs rise as output is increased. Constant returns to scale exist when long-run average costs remain constant as output is increased.

32.   The cost function for a multiproduct firm, denoted $C(Q_1, Q_2)$, defines the cost of producing Q_1 units of good one and Q_2 units of good two, assuming all inputs are used efficiently.

33.   Economies of scope exist when

$$C(Q_1, 0) + C(0, Q_2) > C(Q_1, Q_2);$$

that is, it is cheaper to produce outputs Q_1 and Q_2 jointly than separately.

34.   Let $C(Q_1,Q_2)$ be the cost function for a multiproduct firm, and let $MC_1(Q_1,Q_2)$ be the marginal cost of producing the first output. The cost function exhibits cost complementarity if

$$\frac{\Delta MC_1(Q_1,Q_2)}{\Delta Q_2} < 0;$$

that is, if an increase in the output of product two decreases the marginal cost of producing output one.

35.   The multiproduct cost function

$$C(Q_1,Q_2) = f + aQ_1 Q_2 + (Q_1)^2 + (Q_2)^2$$

has corresponding marginal cost functions

$$MC_1(Q_1, Q_2) = aQ_2 + 2Q_1$$

and

$$MC_2(Q_1, Q_2) = aQ_1 + 2Q_2.$$

36.   The multiproduct cost function

$$C(Q_1,Q_2) = f + aQ_1 Q_2 + (Q_1)^2 + (Q_2)^2$$

    (a)   exhibits cost complementarity whenever $a < 0$;
    (b)   exhibits economies of scope whenever $f - aQ_1 Q_2 > 0$.

Questions: Chapter 5

$MP = \dfrac{DQ}{DL}$

$AP = \dfrac{Q}{L}$

1.   Complete the following table:

K	L	Q	$\dfrac{\Delta Q}{\Delta L} = MP_L$	$\dfrac{Q}{L} = AP_L$
2	0	0	–	–
2	1	50	50	50
2	2	150	100	75
2	3	210	60	70
2	4	240	30	60
2	5	240	0	48
2	6	210	–30	35

(handwritten annotations in table: MP, AP columns; notes "MP rate")

2.   For the linear production function, $Q = 2K + 16L$:

a.   What is the marginal product of capital when the firm uses 3 units of capital and 4
units of labor?   MP $Q = 6 + 64 = 70$

$\dfrac{OQ}{OK} = 2$ $MP = \dfrac{\Delta Q}{\Delta K}$

b.   What is the average product of labor when the firm uses 3 units of capital and 4
units of labor? $AP = \dfrac{Q}{L} = \dfrac{70}{4} = 17.5$

3.   For the Leontief production function, $Q = \text{Min}\{2K, 16L\}$:

a.   How much output is produced when the firm uses 100 units of capital and 0 units
of labor?

0

b.   What is the average product of capital when the firm uses 3 units of capital and 4 units of labor?

4.   For the Cobb-Douglas production function, $Q = K^{.5}L^{.5}$:

a.   What is the marginal product of capital when the firm uses 25 units of capital and 10,000 units of labor?

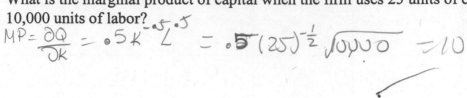

$$MP = \frac{\partial Q}{\partial k} = .5 K^{-.5} L^{.5} = .5 (25)^{-\frac{1}{2}} \sqrt{10,000} = 10$$

b.   What is the average product of capital when the firm uses 25 units of capital and 10,000 units of labor?

$$AP = \frac{P}{K} = \frac{\sqrt{25}\sqrt{10,000}}{25} = 20$$

5.   Use Exhibit 5-1 to answer the following questions:

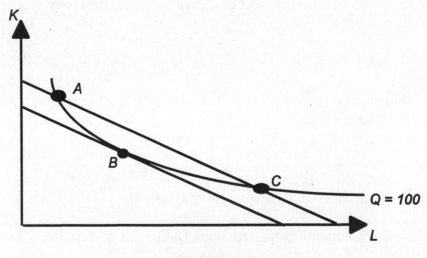

Exhibit 5-1

a. If the firm wishes to produce 100 units of output, what is the cost minimizing combination of capital and labor?

b. Suppose that, at point B, $MP_L = 6$ and $MP_K = 2$. If the firm increases its labor usage by 1 unit and decreases its use of capital by 3 units, what happens to the firm's costs?

6. Suppose the Firm's cost function is given by $C(Q) = 100 + Q + 2Q^2 + 3Q^3$.

a. What are the firm's fixed costs?

$$FC = 100$$

b. What is the firm's variable cost of producing 2 units of output?

$$Q = 2$$
$$VC = 2 + 2(4) + 3(8) = 34$$

c. What is the firm's total cost of producing 2 units of output?

$$134$$

d. How does your answer to c related to your answers in parts a and b?

$$TC = FC + VC$$

e. Calculate the marginal cost of producing 2 units of output.

$$MC = \frac{\partial C}{\partial Q} = 1 + 4Q + 9Q^2 = 1 + 8 + 9(4) = 45$$

f. Calculate the average variable cost of producing 2 units of output.

$$AVC = \frac{VC}{Q} = \frac{34}{2} = 17$$

g. Calculate the average fixed cost of producing 2 units of output.

50

h. Calculate the average total cost of producing 2 units of output.

67

i. Does the minimum point of the ATC curve occur at an output greater or less than 2 units?

Technical Problems: Chapter 5

1. A firm produces output that can be sold at a price of $100. The production function is given by

$P = 100$

$$Q = F(K, L) = K^{1/2} L^{1/2}.$$

a. If capital is fixed at 25 units in the short run, how much labor should the firm $w = 250$ employ in order to maximize profits if the wage rate is $250?

$Q = 5L^{\frac{1}{2}}$

$MP = \dfrac{\partial Q}{\partial L} = \dfrac{5}{2} L^{\frac{1}{2}}$

$\dfrac{500}{2} \dfrac{1}{\sqrt{L}} = 250$

$L = 1$

b. If capital costs $1 per unit, what are the firms total costs?

$25 + 250 = 275$

2. Automated Labs uses 5 workers and 200 machines to produce its product. The marginal product of the last worker is 2 units of output per day; the marginal product of the last machine is 400 units of output per day. Workers are each paid $100 per day, and the rental price of each machine is $300 per day.

a. What is the marginal product per dollar spent on a worker?

b.   What is the marginal product per dollar spent on a machine?

c.   Is Automated Labs utilizing workers and machines in the cost-minimizing manner?

3.   In order to be eligible to attend a biology class, you are required to pay non-refundable tuition fees of $1,000. In addition, you must purchase books from the bookstore at a cost of $200. It costs you $2.00 in bus fare each time you attend class. The bookstore will buy back your books for $100 at the end of the semester.

a.   What are the fixed costs of attending biology class?

Book   200
tuition fees   1000
               1200

b.   What are the variable costs of attending biology class?

2/ fare

c.   What are your sunk costs of attending biology class?

tuition fee = 1000
+ ½ Book   100
               1100

4.   Suppose the production function is Q = K + 2L:

a.   Graph the isoquant corresponding to 4 units of output in Exhibit 5-2.

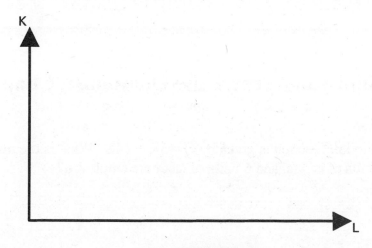

Exhibit 5-2

93

b.   What is the slope of the isoquant?

c.   If the price of labor is $2 per hour and the rental price of capital is $2 per hour, how much capital and labor should be used to minimize the cost of production? Illustrate this in your graph.

5.   Suppose the cost function is C(Q) = 2Q. In Exhibit 5-3 graph the marginal cost curve, average total cost curve, and the average variable cost curve.

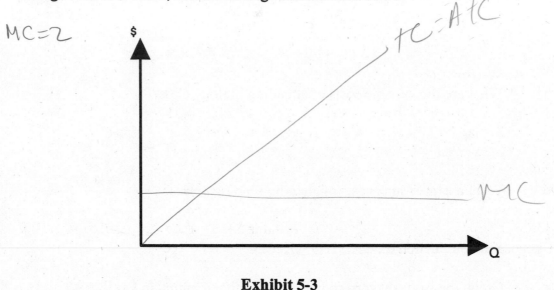

MC=2

$

tc=AtC

MC

Q

Exhibit 5-3

Multiple Choice and True/False Questions: Chapter 5

1.   Suppose the production function is given by Q = 3K + 14L. What is the marginal product of labor when 9 units of capital and 6 units of labor are employed?
      a. 3
      b. 6
      c. 9
      d. 14

MP = $\frac{\Delta Q}{\Delta L}$ $\frac{\partial Q}{\partial L}$

94

2. Suppose the production function is given by $Q = 3K + 4L$. What is the average product of capital when 2 units of capital and 0 units of labor are employed?
   a. 2
   b. 3
   c. 6
   d. none of the above

$AP = \dfrac{Q}{Rent} = \dfrac{6}{2}$

3. If a firm's production function is Leontief and the wage rate goes up
   a. the firm will substitute capital for labor in order to minimize costs
   b. the firm will substitute labor for capital in order to minimize costs
   c. the firm will use more of both inputs to minimize costs
   d. none of the above

4. The change in total cost attributable to the last unit of output is the:
   a. average product
   b. marginal product
   c. marginal cost
   d. average cost

5. It is profitable to alter the utilization of labor if the
   a. value marginal product of labor is less than wage
   b. value marginal product of labor is greater than the wage
   c. both a and b
   d. none of the above

6. If the wage rate is $3 and the price of capital is $4, we know the absolute value of the slope of the isoquant at the point of cost minimization equals
   a. 3/4
   b. 4/3
   c. the capital to labor ratio
   d. b and c

7. An increase in the wage rate causes
   a. the isoquant to become steeper
   b. the isoquant to become flatter
   c. the isocost line to become steeper
   d. the isocost line to become flatter

8. Costs that are forever lost after they have been paid are called
   a. variable costs
   b. fixed costs
   c. sunk costs
   d. none of the above

95

9. The marginal cost curve intersects which of the following curve's minimum point?
   a. Average total cost curve
   b. Average fixed cost curve
   c. Average product curve
   d. All of the above
   e. a and c only

10. True or False: The minimum average cost of producing alternative levels of output, allowing for optimal selection of all variables of production, is defined by the long run average total cost curve.

11. True or False: The short-run is defined as the time-frame in which there are fixed factors of production.

12. True or False: As long as marginal product is increasing, marginal product is greater than average product.

13. True or False: The value of marginal product of an input is the value of the average product of an input.

14. True or False: The Leontief production function implies that, to minimize costs, a firm will use less of an input when its price increases.

15. True or False: The marginal product of labor for the Cobb-Douglas production function is constant, that is, does not vary as the levels of capital and labor vary.

16. True or False: The linear production function exhibits isoquants with a constant marginal rate of technical substitution.

17. True or False: With a Cobb-Douglas production function, an increase in the price of capital will cause a cost minimizing firm to use less capital and more labor.

18. True or False: The marginal cost curve intersects the ATC and AVC curves at their minimum points.

19. True or False: Cost complementary exists in a multiproduct cost function when the marginal cost of producing one output is reduced when the output of another product is increased.

20. True or False: When there are economies of scope between two products which are separately produced by two firms, merging into a single firm can accomplish a reduction in costs.

96

Answers to Questions: Chapter 5

1. Your table should look like this:

K	L	Q	$\frac{\Delta Q}{\Delta L} = MP_L$	$\frac{Q}{L} = AP_L$
2	0	0	-	-
2	1	50	50	50
2	2	150	100	75
2	3	210	60	70
2	4	240	30	60
2	5	240	0	48
2	6	210	-30	35

2.   a.   2

       b.   17.5. To see this, note that $Q = 2(3) + 16(4) = 70$ units, so the $AP_L = 70/4 = 17.5$.

3.   a.   0. This is because $Q = \text{Min } \{2(100), 16(0)\} = \text{Min}\{200, 0\} = 0$.

       b.   2. To see this, note that $Q = \text{Min } \{2(3), 16(4)\} = \text{Min}\{6, 64\} = 6$. Thus, we know $AP_K = 6/3 = 2$.

4.   a.   10. To see this, compute $MP_K = .5 \, K^{-.5}L^{.5} = .5 \, (25)^{-.5}(10,000)^{.5} = .5(25)^{-.5}(100) = 10$.

       b.   20. To see this, compute $Q = K^{.5}L^{.5} = (25)^{.5}(10,000)^{.5} = 5(100) = 500$, so $AP_K = 500/25 = 20$.

5.   a.   Point B.

    b.   The firm's costs would not change. To see this, note that at point B, the MRTS = $MP_L/MP_K = 6/3 = 3$. Since point B is a point of cost minimization, $w/r = 3$. Therefore, if the firm uses 3 units less capital and 1 unit more labor, it remains on the same isocost line.

6.   a.   100

    b.   34. This is because $VC(Q) = Q + 2Q^2 + 3Q^3 = 2 + 2(2)^2 + 3(2)^3 = 34$.

    c.   134. This is because $C(Q) = 100 + Q + 2Q^2 + 3Q^3 = 100 + 2 + 2(2)^2 + 3(2)^3 = 134$.

    d.   Notice that $C = FC + VC$. In other words, your answer in c equals the sum of your answers in a and b.

    e.   45. This is because $MC = 1 + 4Q + 9Q^2 = 1 + 4(2) + 9(2)^2 = 45$.

    f.   17. We calculated the variable cost of 2 units in part b, so $AVC(2) = 34/2 = 17$.

    g.   50. This is because $AFC = FC/Q = 100/2 = 50$.

    h.   67. This is because $ATC = C/Q = 134/2 = 67$.

    i.   Parts e and h reveal that MC < ATC at 2 units of output, so ATC must be falling. Therefore, ATC must achieve its minimum at an output that is greater than 2 units.

Answers to Technical Problems: Chapter 5

1.   a.   1 unit. Since capital is fixed at 25 units, the short-run production function is $Q = 25^{.5}L^{.5} = 5L^{.5}$. The $VMP_L = P \times MP_L = 100 \times .5(5)L^{-.5} = 250L^{-.5}$. Setting this equal to the wage ($250) and solving for L give us $L = 1$.

    b. $275. Compute this as $C = rK + wL = \$1(25) + \$250(1) = \$275$.

2.   a.   .02. Compute this as $MP_L/w = 2/100 = .02$

      b.   1.33. Compute this as $MP_K/r = 400/300 = 1.33$

      c.   No. Since the marginal product per dollar spent on machines exceeds that on labor, Automated Labs is using too many workers and too few machines to minimize the cost of production.

3.   a. $1,200. Your fixed costs are the costs of tuition and books.

      b. $2. The cost each time you visit class is $2.

      c. $1,100. $100 of your fixed costs aren't sunk, since you can recoup $100 when you sell back your books.

4.   a.   Set $4 = K + 2L$, or $K = 4 - 2L$. Your graph should look like curve a in Exhibit 5-4:

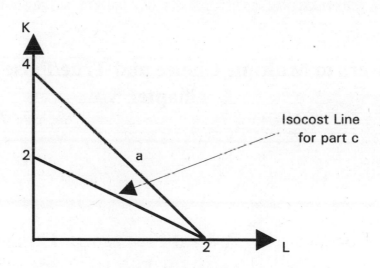

Exhibit 5-4

      b.   -2.

99

c.   You should use 2 units of labor and 0 units of capital, as the graph in Exhibit 5-4 reveals.

5.   See Exhibit 5-5.

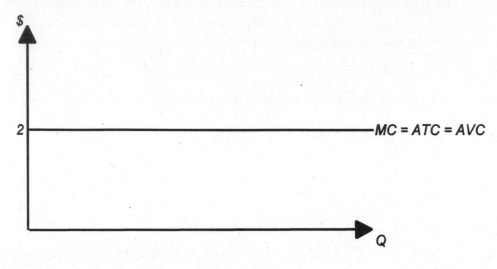

Exhibit 5-5

Answers to Multiple Choice and True/False Questions: Chapter 5

1.   d
2.   b
3.   d
4.   c
5.   c
6.   a
7.   c
8.   c
9.   a
10.   True
11.   True
12.   True
13.   False; price times marginal product
14.   False; there is no substitution with a Leontief technology
15.   False; there is substitution with a Cobb-Douglas technology
16.   True

17.   True
18.   True
19.   True
20.   True

Chapter 6
The Organization of the Firm

Chapter 6 at a Glance

Key Concepts: Chapter 6

1. There are three basic methods managers can use to acquire inputs: spot exchange, contracts, or vertical integration.

2. Spot exchange occurs when the buyer and seller of an input meet, exchange, and then go their separate ways.

3. A contract is a legal document that creates an extended relationship between a particular buyer and seller of an input; it specifies the terms under which they agree to exchange over a given time horizon (say, three years).

4. Vertical integration occurs when a firm shuns other suppliers and chooses to produce an input internally.

5. Optimal input procurement depends on the transactions costs associated with the different methods of acquiring inputs.

6. The transaction costs of acquiring an input are the costs of locating a seller of an input, negotiating a price at which the inputs will be purchased, and putting the input to use. Transactions costs include such things as:
   (a) The cost of searching for a supplier willing to sell a given input;
   (b) The costs of negotiating a price at which the input will be purchased. These costs may be in terms of the opportunity cost of time, legal fees, etc.;
   (c) Other investments and expenditures required to facilitate exchange.

7. A specialized investment (also called a specific investment) is an expenditure that must be made in order for two parties to exchange, but which has little or no value in any alternative use. Examples include site specificity, physical asset specificity, and dedicated assets.

8. Site specificity occurs when the buyer and seller of an input must locate their plants close to one another in order to engage in exchange.

9. Physical asset specificity refers to a situation where the capital equipment needed to produce an input is designed to meet the needs of a particular buyer, and cannot readily be adapted to produce inputs needed by other buyers.

10. Dedicated assets are general investments made by a firm that allow it to exchange with a particular buyer.

11. Specific investments increase transaction costs because they lead to (1) bargaining costs; (2) under investment; and (3) opportunism.

12. Relationship-specific exchange occurs when the parties to a transaction have made specialized investments.

13. When a specialized investment must be made before an input can be acquired, the buyer or seller may attempt to capitalize on the "sunk" nature of the investment by behaving opportunistically. This is known as opportunism (also called the "hold-up problem").

14. Complete contracts eliminate the hold-up problem, but are sometimes costly to write.

15. A contract is incomplete if it does not specify the terms of exchange under all possible scenarios.

16. The optimal contract length will increase when the level of specific investment required to facilitate an exchange increases.

17. A decrease in the complexity of the contracting environment leads to longer optimal contracts.

18. When the desired input does not involve specific investments, the firm can use spot exchange to obtain the input without worrying about opportunism and bargaining costs.

19. By using spot exchange, a firm can specialize in doing what it does best, and does not have to spend money writing contracts or engaging in vertical integration.

20. When substantial specialized investments are required to facilitate exchange, spot exchange results in opportunism, bargaining costs, and under investment, and these transaction costs of using spot exchange can often be reduced by using some other method of acquiring an input. When the contracting environment is simple and the cost of writing a contract is less than the transaction costs associated with spot exchange, it is optimal to acquire the input through a contract. When substantial specialized investments are required and the desired input has complex characteristics that are difficult or costly to specify in a contract, the manager should integrate vertically in order to minimize the cost of acquiring inputs needed for production--provided the costs of integration are not too high.

21. The principal agent problem between the owner of a firm and the manager arises because of the separation of ownership and control. The principal (the owner) does not observe the effort of the agent (the manager), and therefore does not know whether poor profit performance is due to bad luck or lack of managerial effort.

22. The principal agent problem between the owner and the manager can be mitigated by implementing incentive contracts or by relying on external incentives. External incentives include (a) the manager's desire to maintain a good reputation for future job prospects, and (2) the threat of a takeover.

23. The principal agent problem between the manager and workers can be mitigated by (a) profit sharing plans, (b) revenue sharing plans, (c) piece rates, and (d) time clocks and spot checks. Each of these methods has advantages and disadvantages.

Questions: Chapter 6

1. Determine whether the following transactions involve spot exchange, contracts or vertical integration:

   a. Joe, a freshman at Bigtime State, buys an economic textbook from the student bookstore.

      Spot exchange

   b. Publishers, Inc. has a legal obligation to purchase a specified amount of paper each year from a mill owned by a major paper company.

      contract

   c. Joe Smith purchases a box of floppy disks from the local computer store.

      Spot exchange

   d. The Hefty Meat Packing Company slaughters the cattle it raises on the owner's land and sells the meat locally.

      VI

2. Determine whether it would be optimal to use spot exchange, contract, or vertical integration to acquire inputs if:

   a. there are no transactions costs.

   SE

   b. there are no specialized investments

   SE

   c. there are significant specific investments required for exchange, and it is extremely costly to write complete contracts.

   VI

3. Suppose there are significant specialized investments required for exchange, and furthermore, significant gains to specialization. It is relatively easy to specify likely future events. What method of procuring inputs would you use, and why?

   Contract

4. List the primary advantages of using the following methods to circumvent the manager-worker principal agent problem:

   a. revenue sharing plans

   b. time clocks

   c. piece rates

5. List the primary disadvantages of using the following methods to circumvent the manager-worker principal agent problem:

    a. revenue sharing plans

    b. time clocks

    c. piece rates

Technical Problems: Chapter 6

1. Amacon is a bicycle manufacturer that produces approximately five thousand bikes each month. In order to meet that demand, Amacon needs ten thousand rubber tires at its assembly plant on the last Thursday of each month.

    a. What would be the pros and cons of using spot exchange to obtain the tires?

    b. What would be the pros and cons of using a contract to obtain the inputs?

    c. What would be the pros and cons of vertically integrating to obtain the tires?

    d. How would you acquire the tires if you were the manager of Amacon?

2.   Explain why, as an individual shareholder, the structure of management's compensation is
      perhaps more important to your well-being than the dollar amount of that compensation
      (at least within limits).

3.   Use Exhibit 6-1 to answer the following questions.

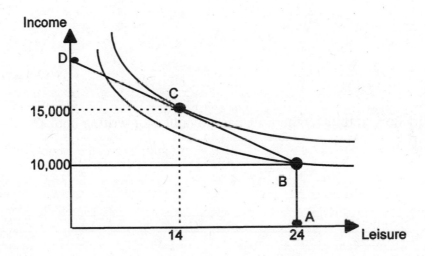

Exhibit 6-1

a. If this manager is paid a fixed salary of $10,000, how much leisure will the manager
    consume during a 24 hour day?

b. When the manager is given a salary of $10,000 plus ten percent of the firm's profits, so that the budget line is ABCD, how much does the manager work in a given 24 hour day?

c. Does the manager prefer $10,000 and 24 hours of leisure, or $15,000 and 14 hours of leisure?

4. a. Why do you think authors are paid royalties for writing books?

b. Are there any disadvantages associated with this type of compensation scheme?

5. A manager is paid $100 per day as a base salary, plus he receives 5 percent of the firm's profits. For every hour he spends managing during an 8 hour day, the firm earns $1,000 in profits. In Exhibit 6-2 graph the manager's opportunity set, and show the situation where he works 7 hours per day, in equilibrium. Also indicate his daily earnings in your graph.

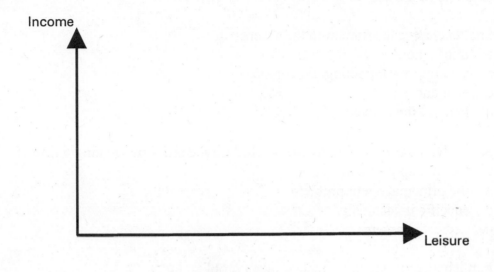

Exhibit 6-2

Multiple Choice and True/False Questions: Chapter 6

1. Managers who cannot physically monitor workers must install incentive or bonus plans to ensure
    a. that the manager will work hard.
    b. that workers will do what the manager wants them to do.
    c. that the owner works hard.
    d. that the company will have positive economic profits

2. Which of the following is a means of avoiding opportunism?
    a. contracts
    b. spot exchange
    c. vertical integration
    d. (a) and (c).

111

3. When relationship-specific exchange occurs in simple contractual environments, the best way to purchase inputs is through
   a. spot markets
   b. vertical integration
   c. short-term agency agreements
   d. none of the above

4. Spot exchange is efficient in the absence of
   a. transactions costs
   b. a complex contracting environment
   c. spot checks
   d. none of the above

5. A disadvantage of separating ownership from control by creating a firm is:
   a. the holdup problem
   b. the principal agent problem
   c. specific investments
   d. dedicated assets

6. Publishers mitigate the principal-agent problem by:
   a. Establishing company-owned authors
   b. Paying their managers very well
   c. Obtaining the most qualified employees
   d. using revenue sharing plans to compensate authors

7. Which of the following provides a manager with an incentive to be an effective manager?
   a. Asset specificity
   b. Dedicated assets
   c. Threat of a takeover
   d. All of the above

8. An example of a job that usually involves a profit sharing plan would be:
   a. Waiters and waitresses
   b. Car salesman
   c. Insurance agents
   d. None of the above

9. The main advantage of a piece rate compensation plan is:
   a. it gives workers an incentive to produce a large quantity of output
   b. it gives workers an incentive to produce output of high quality
   c. it is easy to implement in every production process
   d. none of the above

10. Which type of compensation mechanism does not work through rewards?
    a. Piece rate
    b. Spot check
    c. Revenue sharing
    d. Profit sharing

11. True or False: High transactions costs occur when specialized investment is important.

12. True or False: The principal-agent problem refers to the fact that the agent's goals do not always coincide with those of the principal.

13. True or False: Vertical integration is an efficient way of obtaining inputs when specialized investments are not important.

14. True or False: A spot exchange involves a market where goods are bought and sold at a contracted price.

15. True or False: Long-term contracts reduce opportunistic behavior.

16. True or False: Relationship specific exchange makes spot exchange the best method of input procurement.

17. True or False: By making managerial compensation depend on the performance of the firm's profits, the firm owner's profits fall but social welfare improves.

18. True or False: One problem with revenue-based incentive schemes is they do not generally provide an incentive to maximize profits.

19. True or False: Spot checks work because of the threat of punishment.

Answers to Questions: Chapter 6

1. a.   spot exchange
    b.   contract
    c.   spot exchange
    d.   vertical integration

2. a.   spot exchange or contracts
    b.   spot exchange
    c.   vertical integration

3.   The significant specialized investments required for exchange would lead to underinvestment and a potential holdup problem if spot exchange were utilized. Furthermore, vertical integration would lead to losses due to the lack of specialization in production. Since it is relatively easy to specify likely future events, the optimal method of procuring inputs would be through a contract.

4.   a.   Revenue sharing plans induce agents to maximize revenue, and do not require direct monitoring to do so.

       b.   Time clocks provide workers an incentive to show up on time and to be around at the end of the day.

       c.   Piece rates provide workers with an incentive concentrate on the quantity of output they produce.

5.   a.   Revenue sharing plans do not provide workers an incentive to care about the firm's costs.

       b.   Time clocks do not directly measure the productivity of workers, only physical presence at the workplace.

       c.   Piece rates do not provide workers an incentive to directly care about product quality.

Answers to Technical Problems: Chapter 6

1.   a.   By using spot exchange, Amacon could continue to specialize in doing what it does best -- produce bicycles. Furthermore, it has the flexibility to purchase tires from the seller offering the best price. However, it would be subject to a potential hold-up problem from suppliers, and this might be a problem if there aren't numerous suppliers ready to supply ten thousand rubber tires per month.

       b.   By using a contract, Amacon could continue to specialize in doing what it does best. In addition to these gains from specialization, a contract with a supplier would mitigate the hold-up problem, and entirely eliminate it if the contracting environment is relatively simple. The primary disadvantages of contracts is that they are sometimes costly to write and reduce Amacon's flexibility in purchasing tires from other suppliers.

       c.   Vertical integration would eliminate the hold-up problem and eliminate contracting costs. However, it would probably be expensive to get into the tire business just to be able to obtain 10,000 tires per month. In addition, there would likely be some losses due to Amacon's lack of specialization.

d. Bicycle tires are a relatively standardized product, and 10,000 doesn't seem like too large an amount to find in a month's time. If, after examining the availability of tires in the market I determined they were available in large quantities, I'd use spot exchange. Otherwise, I'd seek out an individual supplier and use a contract in order to eliminate opportunism and the hold-up problem.

2. Fixed payments don't provide managers with sharp incentives, while profit sharing payment schemes do. Therefore, the level of compensation is not as important at generating firm profits (and therefore enhancing shareholder well-being) as the method in which that compensation was earned.

3. a. If the manager is paid a fixed salary of $10,000 equilibrium is at point B in the diagram. The manager consumes 24 hours of leisure during a 24 hour day.

   b. When the manager is given a salary of $10,000 plus ten percent of the firm's profits, so that the budget line is ABCD, equilibrium is at point C in the diagram. The manager consumes 14 hours of leisure in a 24 hour day, which means he works 10 hours per day.

   c. The manager prefers $15,000 and 14 hours of leisure, since the indifference curve through point C lies above the one through point B.

4. a. Publishers can't monitor the effort of authors. By paying royalties, which are a form of revenue sharing, authors have an incentive to write a good book in order to be able to sell lots of them and earn lots in royalties.

   b. With a royalty scheme, the author's objective is to maximize book revenues, while the publishers incentive is to maximize profits. Since profits for the publisher are revenues minus costs, the author might want to include things in the book (like lots of artwork, graphs, pictures, and the like) that enhance revenues but are very costly for the publisher. Therefore, the publisher might not actually maximize profits with this scheme.

5. If the manager consumes 8 hours of leisure in a day, he earns $100. If he works 8 hours, he earns .05 x ($1,000) x 8 = $400 as a bonus, plus the base of $100. Thus if he consumes no leisure, his income is $500. Therefore, the manager's opportunity set looks like the one in Exhibit 6-3 below. Equilibrium is at point F, where he works 7 hours per day. His total compensation (shown on the vertical axis) is computed as .05 x ($1,000) x 7 + $100 = $450.

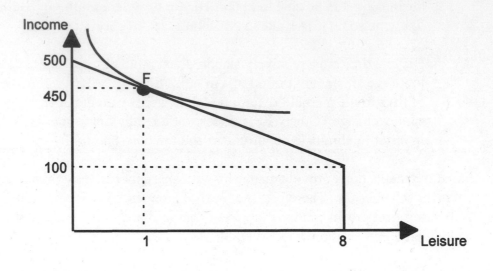

Exhibit 6-3

Answers to Multiple Choice and True/False Questions: Chapter 6

1.   b
2.   d
3.   d
4.   a
5.   b
6.   d
7.   c
8.   d
9.   a
10.   b
11.   True
12.   True
13.   False
14.   False; a market price
15.   True
16.   False
17.   False; the owner's profits rise
18.   True
19.   True

Chapter 7
The Nature of Industry

Chapter 7 at a Glance

Key Concepts: Chapter 7

1. Market structure refers to factors such as the number of firms that compete in the market, the size of the firms (concentration), technological and cost conditions, demand conditions, and at ease with which firms can enter or exit the industry.

2. Concentration ratios provide a measure of how much of the total output in an industry is produced by the largest firms.

3. Let S_1, S_2, S_3, and S_4 denote the sales of the largest four firms in an industry, and let S_T denote the total sales of all firms in the industry. The four-firm concentration ratio is given by

$$C_4 = \frac{S_1 + S_2 + S_3 + S_4}{S_T}.$$

4. The closer to zero the four-firm concentration ratio, the less concentrated is the industry. The closer the index is to one, the more concentrated is the industry.

5. Four firm concentration ratios that are close to zero are indicative of markets where there are many sellers, giving rise to much competition among producers for the right to sell to consumers. Industries with four-firm concentration ratios close to one are indicative of markets in which there is little competition among producers for consumers.

6. Suppose firm i's share of the total market output is $w_i = S_i/S_T$, where S_i is firm i's sales, and S_T is total sales in the industry. Then the Herfindahl-Hirshman index is

$$HHI = 10,000 \cdot \sum w_i^2.$$

7. The value of the Herfindahl-Hirshman index lies between zero and 10,000. A value of 10,000 arises when a single firm (with a market share of 100 percent) exists in the industry. A value of zero results when there are numerous infinitesimally small firms.

8. The Herfindahl-Hirshman index places a greater weight on firms with large market shares than does the four-firm concentration ratio.

9. C_4 and HHI tend to overstate the true level of concentration in markets with significant foreign penetration.

10. C_4 and HHI indices constructed from national data tend to understate the true degree of concentration when the relevant markets are local.

11. C_4 and HHI are sensitive to the definitions of product classes used to define an industry.

12. The Rothschild index is given by

$$R = \frac{E_T}{E_F},$$

where E_T is the elasticity of demand of the total market, and E_F is the elasticity of demand for the product of an individual firm.

13. The Rothschild index takes on a value between zero and one. When the index is one, the individual firm faces a demand curve that has the same sensitivity to price as the market demand curve. When the elasticity of demand for an individual firm's product is much greater (in absolute value) than the elasticity of the market demand, the Rothschild index is close to zero.

14. The Lerner index is given by

$$L = \frac{P - MC}{P},$$

where P is price and MC is marginal cost.

15. In industries where firms rigorously compete for consumers by attempting to charge the lowest price in the market, the Lerner index is close to zero. When firms do not rigorously compete for consumers by price competition, the Lerner index will be closer to one.

16. The markup factor, $1/(1-L)$, defines the factor by which firms multiply marginal cost to set the price of their goods.

17. The Dansby-Willig Performance Index (DW) ranks industries according to how much social welfare would improve if the output in an industry were increased by a small amount.

18. Vertical integration refers to a situation where various stages in the production of a single product are carried out in a single firm.

19. Horizontal integration refers to the merging of the production of similar products into a single firm.

20. Conglomerate merger refers to the merging of different product lines into a single firm.

21. The "causal view" of the structure, conduct, performance paradigm asserts that market structure "causes" firms to behave in a certain way. In turn, this behavior, or conduct, "causes" resources to be allocated in such-and-such a way, leading to either "good" or "poor" market performance.

22. The "feedback critique" asserts that there is not a one-way causal link between structure, conduct, and performance. The conduct of firms can affect market structure; market performance can affect conduct as well as market structure.

Questions: Chapter 7

1. List the 5 major variables that influence market structure, and provide a brief statement indicating why they are important to managers.

   a. Concentration

   b. technology

   c. Ease of entry; exit

   d. # firm xy

   e. Cost, dema ec

2.   Give 4 examples of variables or activities that represent the conduct of firms within an industry.

a.

b.

c.

d.

3.   Determine whether the following are examples of horizontal, vertical, or conglomerate merger:

a.   A luxury car manufacturer merges with the producer of economy cars.

b.   A movie company merges with a firm that produces personal computers.

c.   A car manufacturer merges with a firm that produces steel.

4.   a. What is the Lerner Index?

b. Why is it useful?

5.   a. What is the four-firm concentration ratio?

b. Why is it useful?

c. What are its limitations?

6.   a. What is the Herfindahl-Hirshman index?

      b. Why is it useful?

      c. What are its limitations?

7.   a. What is the Dansby-Willing industry performance index?

      b. Why is it useful?

Technical Problems: Chapter 7

1. Suppose an industry is comprised of 6 firms. Two firms have sales of $100 million each, and four firms have sales of $50 million each. Compute the four-firm concentration ratio for this industry, and explain what it means.

$$C_4 = \frac{100 + 100 + 50 + 50}{400} = .75$$

2. Suppose an industry is comprised of 6 firms. Two firms have sales of $100 million each, and four firms have sales of $50 million each.

   a. Compute the Herfindahl-Hirshman index for this industry.

   $$HHI = \left(\frac{100}{400}\right)^2 + \left(\frac{100}{400}\right)^2 + \left(\frac{50}{400}\right)^2 + \left(\frac{50}{400}\right)^2$$

   b. Why does the index take on a different value than the index you computed in problem 1 above?

3. The industry elasticity of demand for soft drinks is -2, while the elasticity of demand for a representative producer of soft drink is -6.

   a. What is the Rothschild index for this industry?

   b. What does this suggest about the soft drink industry?

4. Firms in the apparel industry have a marginal cost of $5 and charge a price of $15 for a shirt.

    a. What is the Lerner index for this industry?

    b. What is the markup factor for firms in this industry?

5. Do highly concentrated industries necessarily have Lerner indices that are close to 1? Explain.

Multiple Choice and True/False Questions: Chapter 7

1. A firm has a marginal cost of $20 and charges a price of $20. The Lerner index for this firm is:
    a. 0
    b. 1
    c. 20
    d. none of the above

2. The industry elasticity of demand for widgets is -1, while the elasticity of demand for an individual gadget manufacturer's product is -100. Based on the Rothschild approach to measuring market power, we conclude that
    a. there is little monopoly power in this industry.
    b. there is significant monopoly power in this industry.
    c. the Herfindahl index for this industry is -2.
    d. the Herfindahl index for this industry is 2.

3. A Herfindahl index of 10,000 suggests
   a. monopoly.
   b. monopolistic competition.
   c. perfect competition.
   d. oligopoly.

4. Which of the following kinds of market structure are associated with market power:
   a. oligopoly
   b. monopoly
   c. perfect competition
   d. a and b

5. Which of the following is used to measure market structure?
   a. four-firm concentration ratio
   b. HHI (Herfindahl-Hirshman Index)
   c. Dansby-Willig Performance Index
   d. a and b.

6. Based on the following numbers we can conclude that

	Industry A	Industry B
C_4	1	0
HHI	10,000	0

   a. Industry A is a monopoly.
   b. Industry B is a monopoly.
   c. Neither industry is perfectly competitive.
   d. Neither industry is a monopoly.

7. Industries with a Herfindahl index close to _____ are considered to be competitive, while those with values close to _____ are considered non-competitive.
   a. 100000, 0
   b. 0, 10000
   c. 1, 0
   d. 0, 1

8. Four firm concentration ratios and HHIs computed from national data:
   a. will overstate the true level of concentration when there are foreign producers in the market.
   b. will understate the true level of concentration when there are foreign producers in the market.
   c. will overstate the true level of concentration when markets are local.
   d. none of the above.

9. According to the "causal view,"
    a. the conduct of firms in an industry will affect the firm's performance.
    b. the market structure of firms in an industry will affect the conduct of firms.
    c. all of the above
    d. none of the above

10. Which of the following measures performance?
    a. four-firm concentration ratio
    b. Herfindahl-Hirshman Index
    c. the Dansby-Willig Index
    d. all of the above

11. True or False: According to the feedback critique, market structure causes firms to behave in a certain way.

12. True or False: Pricing is an aspect of a firm's conduct.

13. True or False: The Dansby-Willig Index measures the potential for a change in firm profits.

14. True or False: If an electronic company merges with a food company, it would represent conglomerate merger.

15. True or False: A silicon chip maker buying out a computer manufacturer represents vertical merger.

16. True or False: Horizontal merger can enhance the market power of the merging firms.

17. True or False: Of all the market structures, oligopoly has the most market power because it is comprised of several monopolists.

18. True or False: If the four firm concentration ratio indicates that industry A is more concentrated than industry B, then so will the HHI.

19. True or False: The C_4 and HHI indices are generally useful for measuring the performance of an industry.

20. True or False: The four basic market structures are monopoly, perfect competition, monopolistic competition, and oligopoly.

Answers to Questions: Chapter 7

1. a. Firm size. Some industries naturally give rise to larger firms than do other industries.

    b. Industry concentration. The decisions of managers who face little competition within the industry will generally be different from those of managers who face more substantial competitors.

    c. Technology. Differences in technology (eg., whether industries are capital or labor intensive) give rise to differences in production techniques across industries.

    d. Demand and market conditions. The size of market demand influences the number of firms that can be sustained in an industry.

    e. Potential for entry. The ease with which additional firms can enter the market will influence profits and thus managerial decisions.

2. a. Pricing decisions

    b. Integration and merger activity

    c. Research and development decisions

    d. Advertising decisions

3. a. horizontal merger. Luxury cars and economy cars are similar products.

    b. conglomerate merger. Movies and personal computers represent different product lines.

    c. vertical integration. Steel is a key input used to produce cars.

4. a. The Lerner index is $L = (P - MC)/P$, where P is the price charged and MC is the marginal cost of production.

    b. The Lerner index is useful because it provides a measure of pricing conduct of firms in an industry. If the Lerner index is close to 0, then firms charge prices close to marginal cost.

5. a. The four firm concentration ratio is

$$C_4 = \frac{S_1 + S_2 + S_3 + S_4}{S_T}$$

where S_i represents the sales of firm i. Thus, the four-firm concentration ratio tells us the percentage of total industry sales produced by the largest four firms in the industry.

b. A four firm concentration ratio of α tells us that the largest four firms are producing $\alpha \times 100$ percent of the industry's entire output. Thus, C_4 provides a measure of concentration, that is, how concentrated industry output is in the hands of the largest four firms.

c. Because the index does not take into account the market shares of the 5th, 6th (and so on) largest firms, it is not capable of distinguishing differences in concentration of industries that differ only with regard to the composition of the market shares of firms 5 through n. In practice, the index is typically calculated from national data, and therefore (a) overstates the true level of concentration in industries where foreign firms compete, and (b) understates the true concentration in industries where markets are defined locally.

6. a. The Herfindahl-Hirshman index is defined by

$$HHI = 10,000 \cdot \sum_i w_i^2.$$

where w_i is the market share of firm i.

b. The HHI tells us the sum of the squared market shares (times 10,000) of all firms in the industry. If the index is 10,000, then one firm dominates the entire market; if it is 0, then no firm dominates the market. Thus, it provides a measure of concentration which, unlike C_4, takes into account the market shares of all firms in the industry, and by squaring market shares, weights firms with larger market shares more heavily than those with smaller market shares.

c. Like C_4, in practice, the index is typically calculated from national data, and therefore overstates the true level of concentration in industries where foreign firms compete, and understates concentration in industries where markets are defined locally.

7. a. The Dansby-Willing industry performance index ranks industries according to how much social welfare would improve if the output in an industry were increased by a small amount.

    b. It is useful for determining which industry would yield the greatest improvement in welfare if its output were forced to expand by a small amount. This tells regulators interested in imposing restrictions designed to expand industry output which industry is the best target for such regulation.

Answers to Technical Problems: Chapter 7

1. The market share of the largest four firms is $C_4 = \$300/\$400 = .75$. That is, the top four firms produce 75 percent of the industry's output.

2. a. Total industry sales are $400 million, so the market shares of the largest two firms are $w_1 = w_2 = \$100/\$400 = .25$, while the remaining firms have market shares of $w_3 = w_4 = w_5 = w_6 = \$50/\$400 = .125$. Thus, HHI $= 10,000 \times [(.25)^2 + (.25)^2 + (.125)^2 + (.125)^2 + (.125)^2 + (.125)^2] = 1875$.

    b. HHI is based not only the market shares of all 6 firms, but moreover, it squares each market share and thus weights larger firms more heavily than smaller ones.

3. a. $R = E_T/E_F = -2/(-6) = 1/3$.

    b. Individual firms face a demand for their product that is 3 times more elastic than the market demand.

4. a. $L = (P - MC)/P = (\$15 - \$5)/\$15 = 10/15 = 2/3$.

    b. The markup factor is $1/(1 - L) = 1/(1 - 2/3) = 3$. In other words, the price firms charge is 3 times their marginal cost.

5. No. Market structure influences pricing conduct, but does not necessarily imply that firms charge prices that are significantly higher than marginal cost.

Answers to Multiple Choice and True/False Questionns:
Chapter 7

1.   a
2.   a
3.   a
4.   d
5.   d
6.   a
7.   b
8.   a
9.   c
10.   c
11.   False; this is the causal view
12.   True
13.   False; ranks industries according to the potential for improvement in social welfare
14.   True
15.   True
16.   True
17.   False; monopoly has the most market power
18.   False; comparisons may differ using the different indices
19.   False; they measure concentration (an element of structure)
20.   True

Chapter 8
Managing in Competitive, Monopolistic, and Monopolistically Competitive Markets

Chapter 8 at a Glance

Key Concepts: Chapter 8

1.   A market is perfectly competitive if:
   a.   There are many buyers and sellers, each of which is ``small'' relative to the market;
   b.   Each firm in the market produces a homogeneous (an identical) product;
   c.   Buyers and sellers have perfect information;
   d.   There are no transactions costs; and
   e.   There is free entry and exit into the market.

2.   In a perfectly competitive market, the demand curve for an individual firm's product is simply the market price.

3.   Marginal revenue is the change in revenue attributable to the last unit of output. Geometrically, it is the slope of the revenue curve.

4.   The demand curve for a competitive firm's product is a horizontal line at the market price. This price is the competitive firm's marginal revenue:

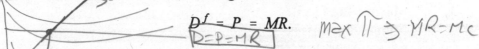

$$D^f = P = MR.$$

5.   In order to maximize profits, a perfectly competitive firm produces the output such that price equals marginal cost in the range where marginal cost is increasing:

$$P = MC(Q).$$

6.   To maximize short-run profits, a perfectly competitive firm should produce in the range of increasing marginal cost where $P = MC$, provided that $P \geq AVC$. If $P < AVC$, the firm should shut down its plant in order to minimize its losses.

7.   The short-run supply curve for a perfectly competitive firm is its marginal cost curve above the minimum point on the AVC curve.

8.   In the long run, perfectly competitive firms produce a level of output such that
   a. $P = MC$;
   b. $P = $ minimum of AC.

9.   A firm is a monopolist if it is the sole supplier in the market of a good for which there are no close substitutes.

10.   Economies of scale exist whenever average total costs decline as total output increases. Diseconomies of scale exist whenever average total costs increase as output increases.

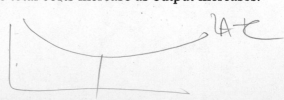

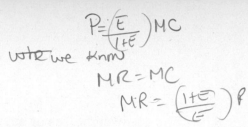

$$P = \left(\frac{E}{1+E}\right)MC$$

where we know

$$MR = MC$$
$$MR = \left(\frac{1+E}{E}\right)P$$

11. The marginal revenue of a monopolist is given by the following formula:

$$MR = P\left[\frac{1 + E}{E}\right],$$

where E is the elasticity of demand for the monopolist's product, and P is the price charged for the product.

12. The inverse demand function, denoted P(Q), indicates the maximum price per unit that consumers would pay for Q units of output.

13. The linear inverse demand function is given by

$$P(Q) = a + bQ,$$

where a is a number greater than zero and b is a number less than zero.

$$TR = P_{(s)} \times Q$$
$$= (a + bQ)Q$$
$$= aQ + bQ^2$$
$$MR = a + 2bQ$$

14. For the linear inverse demand function, marginal revenue is given by

$$MR = a + 2bQ.$$

15. A profit-maximizing monopolist should produce the output, Q^M, such that marginal revenue equals marginal cost:

$$MR(Q^M) = MC(Q^M).$$

16. Given the level of output, Q^M, that maximizes profit, the monopoly price is the price on the demand curve corresponding to the Q^M units produced:

$$P^M = P(Q^M)$$

17. Let MR(Q) be the marginal revenue of producing a total of $Q = Q_1 + Q_2$ units of output. Suppose the marginal cost of producing Q_1 units of output in plant one is $MC_1(Q_1)$ and the marginal cost of producing Q_2 units of output in plant two is $MC_2(Q_2)$. The profit maximizing rule for the two-plant monopolist is to allocate output among the two plants in such a way that

$$MR(Q) = MC_1(Q_1)$$

$$MR(Q) = MC_2(Q_2).$$

$$MC_1 = MC_2$$

133

18.   The deadweight loss of monopoly is the consumer and producer surplus that is lost due to the monopolist charging a price in excess of marginal cost.

19.   An industry is monopolistically competitive if:
       a.   There are many buyers and sellers in the industry;
       b.   Each firm in the industry produces a differentiated product; and
       c.   There is free entry and exit into the industry.

20.   In order to maximize profits, a monopolistically competitive firm produces where its marginal revenue equals marginal cost. The profit-maximizing price is the maximum price per unit that consumers are willing to pay for the profit-maximizing level of output. In other words, the profit-maximizing output, Q^*, is such that

$$MR(Q^*) = MC(Q^*),$$

and the profit-maximizing price is

$$P^* = P(Q^*).$$

21.   In the long run, monopolistically competitive firms produce a level of output such that
       a. $P > MC$;
       b. $P = ATC >$ minimum of average costs.

22.   Niche marketing is a marketing strategy where goods and services are tailored to meet the needs of a particular segment of the market.

23.   Green marketing is a form of niche marketing where firms target products toward consumers who are concerned about environmental issues.

24.   Comparative advertising is a form of advertising where a firm attempts to increase the demand for its brand by differentiating its product from competing brands.

25.   Brand equity refers to the additional value added to a product because of its brand.

26.   To maximize profits, a firm should continue to advertise up to the point where the marginal benefit of advertising equals the marginal cost of advertising.

134

27. The profit-maximizing advertising-to-sales ratio (A/R) is given by

$$\frac{A}{R} = \frac{E_{Q,A}}{-E_{Q,P}},$$

where $E_{Q,P}$ represents the own-price elasticity of demand for the firm's product, $E_{Q,A}$ is the advertising elasticity of demand for the firm's product, A represents the firm's expenditures on advertising, and R = PQ denotes the dollar value of the firm's sales (that is, the firm's revenues).

28. The more elastic the demand for a firm's product, the lower the optimal advertising-to-sales ratio.

29. The greater the advertising elasticity, the greater the optimal advertising-to-sales ratio.

Questions: Chapter 8

1. Explain what would happen to the number of firms in the market in the long run if:

   a.   The market price is $10 and a perfectly competitive firm has average total cost of $12?

   # firms ↓

   b.   The market price is $10 and a perfectly competitive firm has average total cost of $8?

   c.   The price is $10 and a monopolistically competitive firm has average total cost of $12?

   d.   The price is $10 and a monopolistically competitive firm has average total cost of $8?

135

e. The price is $10 and a monopolist has average total cost of $12?

might exit.

f. The price is $10 and a monopolist has average total cost of $8?

stay

2. Answer the following questions based on Exhibit 8-1.

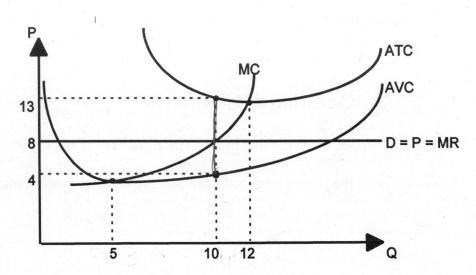

Exhibit 8-1

a. This firm is operates in a *perfect comp* industry.

b. The market price is *8*.

c. The profit maximizing output is *10* units.

d. What are the firm's profits (losses)?

50

e. If the firm shut down, what would it's profits (losses) be?

10 (ATC-AVC) = 10(13-4) = 90

f. In the long run, if conditions in this industry stay the same, will there be entry or exit?

Exit

136

3. Answer the following questions based on Exhibit 8-2.

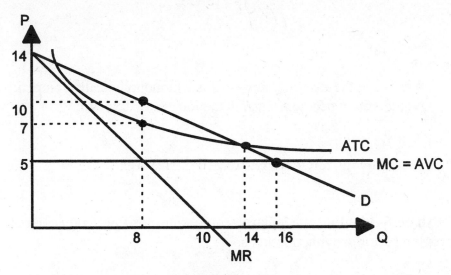

Exhibit 8-2

a. To maximize profits, this firm will produce _____ 8 _____ units.

b. To maximize profits, this firm will charge a price of _____ 10 _____.

c. What are the firm's profits (losses)?

$$\pi = 3 \times 8 = 24$$

d. What is the deadweight loss that arises in this market?

$$\frac{8 \times 5}{2} = 20$$

e. If a perfectly competitive industry faced the same cost and demand conditions, how much output would it produce in the short run?

16

f. If a perfectly competitive industry faced the same cost and demand conditions, how much output would it produce in the long run if it received a subsidy of $16 from the government?

4.   a.   Looking at Exhibit 8-2, can you determine whether the firm in the diagram is a monopolist or a monopolistically competitive firm?

Monopolist

     b.   Assuming the firm in Exhibit 8-2 is a monopolistically competitive firm, what would you expect to happen in the long run? Explain.

↑ Exit until $P = ATC$ ⇒ $\pi = 0$

5.   Use Exhibit 8-3 to illustrate long-run equilibrium for a perfectly competitive firm. Then answer the accompanying questions.

     a.   What is the significance of the relationship between P and MC in the long run?

$P = MC$

     b.   What is the significance of the relationship between P and ATC in the long run?

$P = ATC$

     c.   What is the significance of the relationship between P and the minimum point of the ATC curve in the long run?

at the min ATC

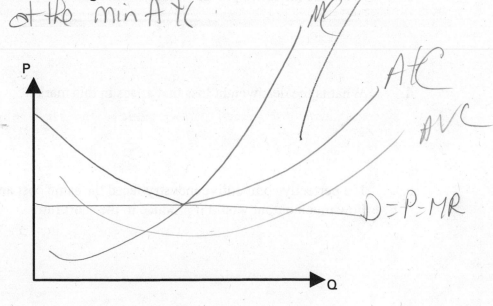

Exhibit 8-3

138

Technical Problems: Chapter 8

1. The cost function for a firm is given by

    $$C(Q) = 5 + Q^2.$$

    The firm sells output in a perfectly competitive market, and other firms in the industry sell output at a price of $40. $P=40$

    a. What price should the manager of this firm put on its product?

    $$40$$

    b. What level of output should be produced to maximize profits?
    $MR=P=40$
    $MC=2Q$

    MC = MR
    40 = 2Q
    Q = 20

    c. How much profits will be earned?

    $$40 \times 20 - (5 + 20^2) = 395$$
    405

    d. Would you expect the profits to remain in the long-run?

    No $\pi = 0$

2. Suppose the inverse demand function and cost function for a <u>monopolist</u>'s product are given by

    $$P = 5 - Q.$$

    $$C(Q) = 3Q$$

    a. If the firm wishes to maximize total revenue, how much output should it produce?

    $P = 5 - Q$ $TR = 5Q - Q^2$
    $MR = 5 - 2Q$

    $5 = 2Q$
    $Q = 2.5$

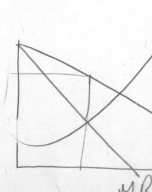

b.　If the firm wishes to maximize total revenue, what price should it charge?

$$P = 2.5$$

c.　At the revenue maximizing level of output and price, what is the elasticity of demand for the firm's product.

$$E = -1$$

$P = 5 - q$
$C = 3q$
$TR = 5q - q^2$
C

d.　If the firm wishes to maximize profits, how much output should it produce?

to max π　　　　MR = MC
MR = MC　　　　$5 - 2q = 3$
MR = 5 - 2q　　　　$q = 1$
MC = 3

e.　If the firm wishes to maximize profits, what price should it charge?

$$P = 5 - 1 = 4$$

f.　What are the firm's maximum profits?

$$TR - C$$
$$4 \times 1 - 3 = 1$$

g.　How much output would a perfectly competitive industry produce given the same demand and cost conditions?

$$P = MR = MC$$
$$P = 3$$
$$3 = 5 - q$$
$$q = 2$$

140

3. Suppose the inverse demand for a monopolist's product is given by

$$P(Q) = 10 - 0.5Q.$$

The monopolist can produce output in two plants. The marginal cost of producing in plant one is $MC_1 = Q_1$, while the marginal cost of producing in plant two is $MC_2 = 2Q_2$.

a. How much output should be produced in each plant to maximize profits?

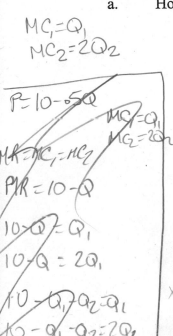

$MC_1 = Q_1$
$MC_2 = 2Q_2$

$P = 10 - 0.5Q$

$MR = MC_1 = MC_2$
$MR = 10 - Q$

$10 - Q = Q_1$
$10 - Q = 2Q_1$

$10 - Q_1 - Q_2 = Q_1$
$10 - Q_1 - Q_2 = 2Q_2$

$10 - 2Q_1 - Q_2 = 0$
$10 - Q_1 - 3Q_2 = 0$

$20 - 2Q_1 - 6Q_2$
$-10 + Q_1 + 5Q_2 = 0$

$Q_2 = 1$
$Q_1 = 4$

$10 - 2Q_1 - 4 = 0$
$6 = 2Q_1$

Max $\pi \Rightarrow$ MR=MC
MR $= MC_2$

$TR = (10 - 0.5(Q_1 + Q_2))(Q_1 + Q_2)$
$= 10(Q_1 + Q_2) - 0.5(Q_1 + Q_2)^2$

$MR_1 = 10 - (Q_1 + Q_2)$

$MC_1 = Q_1$ | MC_2
$10 - Q_1 - Q_2 = Q_1$ | $10 - Q_1 - Q_2 = 2Q_2$

$10 = 2Q_1 + Q_2$
x-2 | $10 = Q_1 + 3Q_2$

$10 = 2Q_1 + Q_2$
$-20 = -2Q_1 - 6Q_2$
_____
$-10 = -5Q_2$

$MR = 10 - Q$

$10 - Q = Q$ | $10 - Q = 2Q$
$10 = 2Q$ | $\frac{10}{3} = Q$
$Q = 5$

$Q_2 = 2$
$Q_1 = 4$

b. What is the firm's total output?

6

c. What price should the firm charge for it's product to maximize profits?

$P = 10 - \frac{1}{2}Q$
$P = 10 - \frac{1}{2}(Q_1 + Q_2)$
$TR = 10(Q_1 + Q_2) - \frac{1}{2}(Q_1 + Q_2)^2$
$MR_1 = 10 - 1(Q_1 + Q_2)$
$10 - (Q_1 + Q_2) = Q_1$
$10 = 2Q_1 + Q_2$

$M_2 = 10 - (Q_1 + Q_2)$

$10 - (Q_1 + Q_2) = 2Q_2$
$10 = Q_1 + 3Q_2$
$20 = 2Q_1 + 6Q_2$

141

$P = 10 - .5(6)$
$= 7$

$10 = 2Q_1 + Q_2$
$20 = 2Q_1 + 6Q_2$
_____
$-10 = -5Q_2$
$Q_2 = 2$
$Q_1 = 4$

4. Suppose the demand function facing a monopolistically competitive firm is given by

$$Q = 10 - 2P.$$

a. Find the inverse demand function.

$$2P = 10 - Q$$
$$P = 5 - \frac{1}{2}Q$$

b. Find the marginal revenue function.

$$MR = 5 - Q$$

c. Determine the output and price at which demand is unitary elastic.

max Revenue

let MR = 0

$$\underline{5 = Q} \qquad \underline{P = 2.5}$$

d. At what quantities is demand elastic?

$$< 5$$

e. At what quantities is demand inelastic?

$$> 5$$

5. Explain why it is sometimes said that, in the long-run, a monopolistically competitive industry has too many firms producing too many products.

6.   A specialty store obtains its product from a foreign manufacturer at constant marginal cost. In an attempt to boost profits, the manager hired an economist to estimate the demand for its product. The economist found that the demand for its product is log-linear, with an own price elasticity of demand of -5 and an advertising elasticity of demand of 1.0. To maximize profits, what fraction of revenues should the firm spend on advertising?

Multiple Choice and True/False Questions: Chapter 8

1.   Which of the following is false?
a.   A monopolist produces on the inelastic portion of its demand.
b.   A monopolist may earn zero economic profit.
c.   The more elastic the demand, the closer marginal revenue is to price.
d.   In the short run a monopoly will shut down if P < AVC.

2.   You are the manager of a monopoly that faces a demand curve described by P = 5 - 5Q. Your costs are C = 1. The profit-maximizing output for your firm is
a. 1/2
b. 1
c. 5
d. none of the above

$MC = 0$

$MR = 5 - 10Q$

$10Q = 5$

$Q = \frac{1}{2}$

143

3. You are the manager of a firm that can sell each additional unit of output produced at a price of $5 per unit. Based on this we can conclude that you operate
   a. a monopoly.
   b. a monopolistically competitive firm.
   c. either a or b.
   d. none of the above.

4. Which of the following is true under monopolistic competition in the long run?
   a. Profits are positive because P > minimum of ATC.
   b. P > minimum of ATC
   c. P = MR
   d. All of the above are true.

5. In the long-run, perfectly competitive firms:
   a. charge prices equal to marginal cost.
   b. have excess capacity.
   c. produce at the minimum of average total cost.
   d. a. and c.

6. If a monopolistically competitive firm's marginal cost declines, then in order to maximize profits the firm will
   a. reduce output and increase price.
   b. increase output and decrease price.
   c. increase both output and price.
   d. reduce both output and price

7. The primary difference between monopoly and monopolistic competition is
   a. the ease of entry and exit into the industry.
   b. the number of firms in the market.
   c. All of the above
   d. None of the above

8. Which of the following is the best example of a perfectly competitive firm?
   a. A farmer in Iowa.
   b. A local utility in a small town.
   c. A newspaper in New York City.
   d. A toothpaste manufacturer.

9. There is no supply curve
   a. for a competitive firm
   b. for a competitive industry
   c. for a monopolistically competitive industry.
   d. none of the above.

144

10. True or False: If profits are negative in a monopolistically competitive industry, in the long run firms will exit and the market supply curve will shift to the left.

11. True or False: A monopolist always earns positive economic profits.

12. True or False: For a perfectly competitive firm, P = MR in both the short run and the long run.

13. True or False: In long-run equilibrium, the output in a monopolistically competitive industry corresponds to that at which average cost is minimized.

14. True or False: A perfectly competitive firm earns zero accounting profits in the long run.

15. True or False: For a monopolist, P > MC in both the long and short runs.

16. In long-run competitive equilibrium, firms have plants of the optimum size.

17. True or False: If firms in a perfectly competitive market are initially making zero economic profits, and if market demand falls, in the long run firms will exit the industry, putting upward pressure on the market price.

18. True or False: A market may be monopolistic because there are some legal barriers to entry.

19. True or False: There is deadweight loss in markets served by monopolists as well as in markets served by monopolistically competitive firms.

Answers to Questions: Chapter 8

1. a. The number of firms would fall. P = $10 < ATC = $12, so firms are earning short run losses and would exit in the long run.

    b. The number of firms would rise. P = $10 > ATC = $8, so firms are earning profits in the short run and new firms would enter in the long run.

    c. The number of firms would fall. P = $10 < ATC = $12, so firms are earning losses in the short run and would exit in the long run.

d.   The number of firms would rise. P = $10 > ATC = $8, so firms are earning profits in the short run and new firms would enter in the long run.

e.   In the absence of any subsidy from the government, the monopolist would exit the industry and the market would cease to exist. P = $10 < ATC = $12, so the monopolist is earning losses in the short run and would leave the industry in the long run.

f.   The number of firms would remain unchanged. While the firm is earning profits, entry barriers keep other firms out of the market.

2.   a.   perfectly competitive, since P = MR.

b. $8.

c.   10 units, since P = MC at 10 units of output.

d.   Losses = $50, computed as (P - ATC) x Q = ($8 - $13) x 10.

e.   The firm would lose $90. The loss if the firm shut down corresponds to its fixed costs, which can be calculated as the (ATC - AVC) x Q. Using the numbers corresponding to Q = 10, we see that these fixed costs are ($13 - $4) x 10 = $90.

f.   exit.

3.   a.   8 units, the point where MR = MC.

b. $10, which is the maximum price consumers will pay for 8 units.

c. $24, computed as (P - ATC) x Q = ($10 - $7) x 8.

d. $20, computed as .5 ($10 - $5) x (16 - 8).

e.   16 units. This corresponds with the point where P = MC. Notice that MC = AVC since MC is flat. Therefore, the price of $5 covers variable costs, so firms will not shut down in the short run.

f.   16 units. A perfectly competitive industry would produce where P = MC. However, this corresponds with an output of 16 units, and at this output profits are negative. In fact, the losses exactly equal the firms's fixed costs, which are (ATC - AVC) x Q = ($7 - $5) x 8 = $16. (Recall, fixed costs do not vary with output, so the fixed costs at 16 units must be the same as those at 8 units). Since the subsidy of $16 exactly offsets these fixed costs, we conclude that firms in a perfectly competitive industry would produce 16 units in the long run, and earn zero economic profits.

4.　a.　No; both monopolists and monopolistically competitive firms face downward sloping demands, and can have cost functions of various shapes. However, the declining average total cost curve indicates economies of scale, which is often indicative of monopoly when demand is small.

　　b.　Since the firm is earning positive economic profits, in the long run new firms would enter. This would reduce the demand for the firm's product until its profits were zero.

5.　Your diagram should look like the one in Exhibit 8-4:

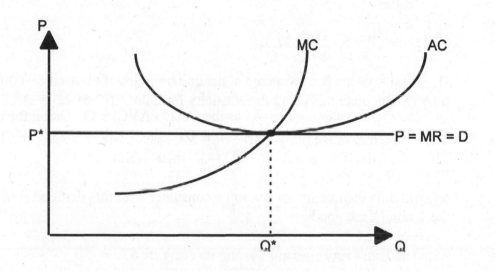

Exhibit 8-4

　　a.　P = MC implies that the value to society of an additional unit of output (P) equals the cost to society of producing another unit (MC). Therefore, the socially efficient level of output is being produced.

　　b.　P = ATC implies that firms are making zero economic profits; there is no incentive for additional firms to enter the market, nor for existing firms to leave the market.

　　c.　P = minimum ATC implies that firms are producing the output corresponding to the optimal plant size. In other words, all economies of scale have been fully exploited.

147

Answers to Technical Problems: Chapter 8

1.   a. $40, which is the market price.

        b.   20 units. To calculate this, set P = MC, or $40 = 2Q. Solving for Q gives Q = 20.

        c. $395. The firm's revenues are P x Q = ($40)(20) = $800. The firm's costs are $C(Q) = 5 + Q^2 = 5 + (20)^2 = \$405$. Profits are thus $800 - $405 = $395.

        d.   No. Additional firms would enter, driving down the market price until profits were zero.

2.   a.   2.5 units. To maximize total revenue set MR = 0. Here, MR = 5 - 2Q, so 5 - 2Q = 0 implies Q = 2.5.

        b. $2.5, since P = 5 - 2.5 = $2.5.

        c.   -1. Total revenue is maximized at the unitary point of elasticity. You can also directly calculate this using the elasticity formula: -1(2.5)/2.5 = -1.

        d.   1 unit. To maximize profits, set MR = MC. Here, MR = 5 - 2Q and MC = 3. Thus, we solve the equation 5 - 2Q = 3, which yields Q = 1.

        e. $4, which is the maximum amount a consumer with this demand function will pay for 1 unit of the good.

        f. $1. The firm's revenues are $4, and its costs are $3.

        g.   2 units. To see this, notice that a competitive industry would produce where P = MC, or in this case, where 5 - Q = 3. Solving this equation gives Q = 2.

3.   a. $Q_1 = 4$ units and $Q_2 = 2$ units. To maximize profits, the firm sets $MR = MC_1$ and $MR = MC_2$. Here, $MR = 10 - (Q_1 + Q_2)$. Thus, the profit maximizing output at each plant satisfies these two conditions:

$$10 - (Q_1 + Q_2) = Q_1$$

$$10 - (Q_1 + Q_2) = 2Q_2.$$

Solving these equations simultaneously gives us $Q_1 = 4$ and $Q_2 = 2$.

b.   6 units, since $Q_1 + Q_2 = 6$.

c. $7, since the maximum price consumers will pay for 6 units of output is $10 - .5(6)$ = $7.

4.   a.   Solve for P in terms of Q to get $P = 5 - .5Q$.

        b. $MR = 5 - Q$. Make sure you use the inverse demand function in part a to get this.

        c. $Q = 5$, $P = 2.5. Demand is unitary elastic at the point where $MR = 0$. Find the corresponding Q by setting $MR = 0$, which implies $5 - Q = 0$. Solve this to get $Q = 5$. Next, use the inverse demand function to see that when $Q = 5$, $P = 2.5.

        d.   Looking at Figure 8-13 of the textbook, we can conclude that demand is elastic for quantities below 5 units.

        e.   Looking at Figure 8-13 of the textbook, we can conclude that demand is inelastic for quantities beyond 5 units.

5.   In the long-run a monopolistically competitive industry has excess capacity. The fact that numerous other firms produce slightly differentiated products means the firm can't profitably expand its own output to fully exploit economies of scale.

6.   To find the profit-maximizing advertising-to-sales ratio, we simply plug $E_{Q,P} = -5$ and $E_{Q,A} = 1.0$ into the formula for the optimal advertising-to-sales ratio:

$$\frac{A}{R} = \frac{E_{Q,A}}{-E_{Q,P}} = \frac{1.0}{5} = 0.20$$

Thus, the optimal advertising-to-sales ratio is 20 percent -- to maximize profits, the firm should spend 20 percent of its revenues on advertising.

Answers to Multiple Choice and True/False Questions: Chapter 8

1.   a
2.   a
3.   d
4.   b
5.   d

6.   b
7.   c
8.   a
9.   c
10.   False; the firm's demand curve shifts to the right.
11.   False
12.   True
13.   False
14.   False, zero economic profits
15.   True
16.   True
17.   True
18.   True
19.   True

Chapter 9
Basic Oligopoly Models

Chapter 9 at a Glance

Key Concepts: Chapter 9

1. Oligopoly refers to an industry comprised of a few firms, each of which is large relative to the total industry. An oligopoly comprised of only two firms is called a duopoly.

2. An industry is characterized as a Sweezy oligopoly if:

    a. There are few firms in the market serving many consumers;

    b. The firms produce differentiated products;

    c. Each firm believes that rivals will cut their prices in response to a price reduction, but will not raise their prices in response to a price increase; and

    d. Barriers to entry exist.

3. An industry is characterized as a Cournot oligopoly if:

    a. There are few firms in the market serving many consumers;

    b. The firms produce either differentiated or homogeneous products;

    c. Each firm believes that rivals will hold their output constant if it changes its output; and

    d. Barriers to entry exist.

4. The reaction function defines the profit-maximizing level of output for a firm for given output levels of the other firm. More formally, the profit-maximizing level of output for Firm One, given that Firm Two produces Q_2 units of output, is given by

$$Q_1 = r_1(Q_2).$$

Similarly, the profit-maximizing level of output for Firm Two, given that Firm One produces Q_1 units of output, is given by

$$Q_2 = r_2(Q_1).$$

5.   Cournot equilibrium is the situation where neither firm has an incentive to change its output, given the output of the other firm. This corresponds to the intersection of the reaction curves.

6.   If the (inverse) demand in a homogeneous product Cournot duopoly is

$$P = a - b(Q_1 + Q_2),$$

then the marginal revenue of Firms One and Two are:

$$MR_1(Q_1, Q_2) = a - bQ_2 - 2bQ_1$$
$$MR_2(Q_1, Q_2) = a - bQ_1 - 2bQ_2.$$

[handwritten notes:]

$$TR = (a - b(Q_1 + Q_2))Q_1$$
$$MR_1 = a - bQ_2 - 2bQ_1$$
$$MC_1 = c_1$$

Max π

$$a - bQ_2 - 2bQ_1 = c_1$$
$$\frac{-2bQ_1}{-2b} = \frac{c_1 - a + bQ_2}{-2b}$$
$$= \frac{a - c_1}{2b} - \frac{1}{2}Q_2$$

7.   For the linear (inverse) demand function

$$P = a - b(Q_1 + Q_2),$$

and cost functions

$$C_1(Q_1) = c_1 Q_1$$
$$C_2(Q_2) = c_2 Q_2,$$

the reaction functions are

$$Q_1 = r_1(Q_2) = \frac{a - c_1}{2b} - \frac{1}{2}Q_2$$
$$Q_2 = r_2(Q_1) = \frac{a - c_2}{2b} - \frac{1}{2}Q_1.$$

8.   A firm's isoprofit curve is defined as the combinations of outputs produced by all firms that yields the firm the same level of profit.

9.   An industry is characterized as a Stackelberg oligopoly if:

   a.   There are few firms in the market serving many consumers;

   b.   The firms produce either differentiated or homogeneous products;

c. A single firm (the leader) selects an output before all other firms choose their outputs;

d. All other firms (the followers) take as given the output of the leader, and choose outputs that maximize profits given the leader's output;

e. Barriers to entry exist.

10. For the linear (inverse) demand function

$$P = a - b(Q_1 + Q_2),$$

and cost functions

$$C_1(Q_1) = c_1 Q_1$$
$$C_2(Q_2) = c_2 Q_2,$$

the follower sets output according to the Cournot reaction function

$$Q_2 = r_2(Q_1) = \frac{a - c_2}{2b} - \frac{1}{2} Q_1.$$

The leader's output is

$$Q_1 = \frac{a + c_2 - 2c_1}{2b}.$$

11. An industry is characterized as a Bertrand oligopoly if:

a. There are few firms in the market serving many consumers;

b. The firms produce identical products at a constant marginal cost;

c. Firms engage in price competition, and react optimally to prices charged by competitors;

d. Consumers have perfect information and there are no transactions costs;

e. Barriers to entry exist.

154

12. A market is contestable if:

    a.   all producers have access to the same technology;

    b.   consumers respond quickly to price changes;

    c.   existing firms cannot respond quickly to entry by lowering price; and

    d.   there are no sunk costs.

Questions: Chapter 9

1. Determine the type of oligopoly that most closely matches the following scenarios:

    a.   Firm A sets its output on the first day of each month. Firm B observes firm A's output, and sets its own output on the second day of each month.

        Stackelberg

    b.   Firms A and B each set their own output, not knowing the output the other firm has set.

        Cournot

    c.   Firms A and B each set their own price, not knowing the price the other firm set.

        Bertrand

    d.   Firm A thinks that it's rival will match its price reductions, but not match its price increases.

2. Exhibit 9-1 shows the demand for a duopolist's product, depending on whether its rival (which produces a slightly differentiated product) matches or does not match its price changes. Suppose we are starting from point E in the diagram.

    a.   What is the firm's demand curve if the rival matches price cuts, but does not match price increases?

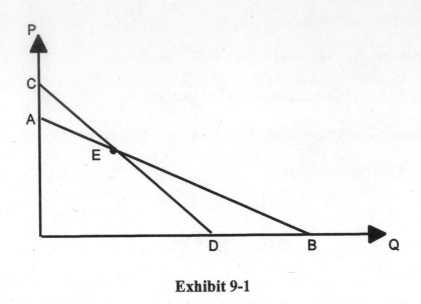

Exhibit 9-1

b.   What is the firm's demand curve if the rival matches price increases, but not price cuts?

3.   Answer the following questions based on the reaction functions and isoprofit curves shown in Exhibit 9-2.

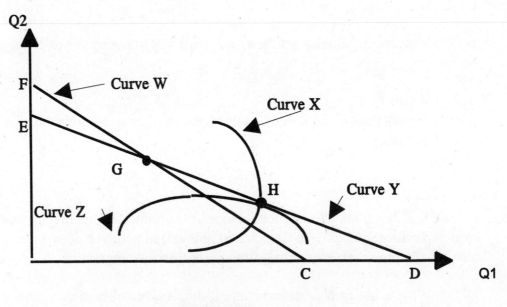

Exhibit 9-2

a.   Which curve represents Firm One's Cournot reaction function?

b.   Which curve represents Firm Two's Cournot reaction function?

c.   Which point represents Firm One's monopoly output?

d.   Which point represents Firm Two's monopoly output?

e.   Which curve represents an isoprofit curve for Firm One?

f.   Which curve represents an isoprofit curve for Firm Two?

g.   Which point represents Cournot equilibrium?

h.   Which point represents a Stackelberg equilibrium?

i.   Considering your answer to the question h, which firm is the leader?

4.   Suppose two firms compete in a homogeneous product market and produce at constant marginal cost of $5.

a.   What prices would be charged in a Bertrand oligopoly? Why?

b.   What price would prevail if the market were perfectly competitive?

5.   a.   Illustrate in Exhibit 9-3 what happens to the output of Firm One if it's marginal cost rises in a Cournot oligopoly.

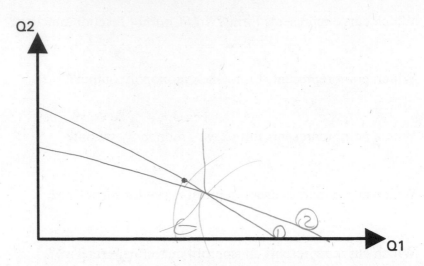

Exhibit 9-3

b.   Illustrate in Exhibit 9-4 what happens to the output of Firm One if it's marginal cost rises in a Sweezy oligopoly.

Exhibit 9-4

6.   Cleaning, Inc. is the only firm in the market that provides housecleaning services. Yet, it earns zero economic profits and charges a price that equals its marginal cost of cleaning a houses.

   a.   Is Cleaning, Inc. a monopolist?

   yes   *No*

   b.   Why do you think Cleaning, Inc. charges a price equal to marginal cost?

   |

Technical Problems: Chapter 9

1.   Suppose the inverse market demand function for two Cournot duopolists is given by:

$$P = 5 - (Q_1 + Q_2)$$

and that their marginal costs are each $1.

   a.   Do the firms produce homogeneous products?

   b.   What is Firm One's marginal revenue?

   $MR_1 = 5 - Q_2 - 2Q_1$ $MC = MR$

   c.   What is Firm One's reaction function?

   $1 = 5 - Q_2 - 2Q_1$

   $2Q_1 = 4 - Q_2$ $Q_1 = 2 - \frac{1}{2}Q_2$

$P = 5 - (Q_1 + Q_2)$

$MC = 1$

$MR_2 = 5 - Q_1 - 2Q_2$

MC_2

d. What is Firm Two's reaction function?

$$Q_2 = \frac{4 - Q_1}{2 \quad 2} = 2 - \frac{1}{2}Q_1$$

e. What are the Cournot equilibrium outputs?

$$Q_1 = 2 - \frac{1}{2}Q_2$$

$$Q_2 = 2 - \frac{1}{2}Q_1$$

$$Q_1 = 2 - \frac{1}{2}\left[2 - \frac{1}{2}Q_1\right]$$

$$= 2 - 1 + \frac{1}{4}Q_1$$

$$\frac{3}{4}Q_1 = 1 \qquad Q_1 = 4/3, \quad Q_2 = 4/3$$

f. What is the Cournot equilibrium price?

$$P = 5 - \left(\frac{8}{3}\right) = \frac{15}{17} \qquad P = 5 - \frac{8}{5} = \frac{25 - 8}{25} = \frac{17}{25}$$

$$= \frac{7}{13}$$

2. Suppose the inverse demand function for two duopolists is given by:

$$P = 5 - (Q_1 + Q_2) \qquad a = 5 \qquad b = -1$$

$$\overset{a}{P} = 5 - (Q_1 + Q_2) \qquad \overset{b}{}$$

$$MC_1 = 1$$

$$MC_2 = 1$$

and that their marginal costs are each \$1. Suppose Firm One is the Stackelberg Leader, and Firm Two is the follower.

a. What is the Leader's equilibrium output?

$$Q_1 = \frac{a + C_2 - 2C_1}{2b} = \frac{5 + 1 - 2}{-2} =$$

b.   What is the Follower's equilibrium output?

$$Q_2 = \frac{a - c_2}{2b} - \frac{1}{2}Q_1 = \frac{5-1}{2} - \frac{1}{2}(2)$$
$$= 2 - 1 = 1$$

c.   What is total market output?

3

d.   What is the equilibrium price?

$$P(5-3) = 7$$

3.   Suppose the inverse demand function for two Bertrand duopolists is given by:

$$P = 5 - (Q_1 + Q_2)$$

and that their marginal costs are each $1.

a.   What is the Bertrand equilibrium price?

1

b.   What is the total market output in the Bertrand equilibrium?

$$1 = 5 - Q$$
$$Q = 4$$

4.   Suppose the inverse market demand function is given by:

$$P = 5 - Q$$

and that its marginal cost is $1.

$$MC = MR$$
$$MR = 5 - 2Q$$

a.   What is the collusive quantity?

$$5 - 2Q = 1$$
$$Q = 2$$
$$P = 3$$

b.   What is the collusive price?

5.   Given the identical demand and cost conditions used in problems 2-4 above, what do you conclude about the total market output and price in the Cournot, Stackelberg, Bertrand and collusive models?

Multiple Choice and True/False Questions: Chapter 9

1. If firms compete in a Bertrand oligopoly, then
    a.   each firm views the output of the rival as given.
    b.   each firm views the prices of rivals as given.
    c.   each firm views the profits of rivals as given.
    d.   all of the above

2.   With linear demand and constant marginal cost, a Stackelberg follower's profits are
            _____ the leader's.
    a   less than
    b.   equal to
    c.   greater than
    d.   twice as great as those of

3. Which of the following is a feature of Sweezy oligopoly?
   a. There is one firm in the market serving many consumers.
   b. Firms produce homogenous products.
   c. Each firm believes that rivals will raise their prices in response to a price reduction, but will not raise their prices in response to a price increase.
   d. none of the above.

4. Two duopolists coexist in a market earning positive economic profits. Neither firm changes its price in response to day to day fluctuations in marginal cost. Based on this, the two firms are most likely competing in
   a. a Sweezy oligopoly.
   b. a Cournot oligopoly.
   c. a Stackelberg oligopoly.
   d. a Bertrand oligopoly.

5. One important condition for a contestable market is
   a. all producers have different technologies.
   b. consumers respond slowly to a price change.
   c. existing firms can respond quickly to entry by lowering their price.
   d. there are no sunk costs.

6. The market demand in a Bertrand duopoly is $P = 10 - Q_1 - Q_2$, and the marginal costs are $0. Fixed costs are zero for both firms. Which of the following statement(s) is/are true?
   a. $P = \$0$
   b. Both firms earn positive profits.
   c. The duopoly results in deadweight loss.
   d. All of the above are true.

7. Which of the following is a condition for a Stackelberg oligopoly?
   a. There are few firms in the industry.
   b. Barriers to entry exist.
   c. A single firm (the leader) selects an output before all other firms choose their outputs.
   d. The firms produce either differentiated or homogeneous products.
   e. All of the above are conditions for Stackelberg oligopoly.

8. From a consumer's point of view, which type of market structure is least desirable?
   a. Bertrand
   b. Cournot
   c. Stackelberg
   d. Monopoly

163

9. A firm's marginal revenue curve jumps down at 50 units of output. This would be not be surprising if the firm competed in a _____ oligopoly.
   a. Sweezy
   b. Cournot
   c. Stackelberg
   d. Bertrand

10. Which would you expect to make the lowest profits, other things equal?
    a. Homogeneous product Bertrand oligopolist
    b. Cournot oligopolist
    c. Stackelberg leader
    d. Stackelberg follower

11. True or False: In Bertrand oligopoly each firm believes that their rivals will hold their output constant if it changes its output.

12. True or False: In Cournot oligopoly firms produce an identical product at a constant marginal cost and engage in price competition.

13. True or False: In oligopoly a change in marginal cost never has an effect on output or price.

14. True or False: The Bertrand model of oligopoly reveals that perfectly competitive prices can arise in markets with only a two firms.

15. True or False: Firms set quantities in Cournot oligopoly, but not in a Stackelberg oligopoly.

16. True or False: A firm's isoprofit curve is defined as the combinations of the outputs produced by all firms that yield the firm the same level of profit.

17. True or False: If there are only two firms in a market, the market price must be above marginal cost.

18. True or False: If there is only one firm in a market, the market price must be above marginal cost.

19. In Stackelberg oligopoly each firm believes that their rivals will hold their output constant if it changes its output.

20. Firms in a Cournot duopoly would experience lower profits if their marginal production costs increased.

164

Answers to Questions: Chapter 9

1.   a.   Stackelberg. Firm A is the leader, firm B the follower.

     b.   Cournot.

     c.   Bertrand.

     d.   Sweezy.

2.   a.   AED.

     b.   CEB.

3.   a.   Curve W.

     b.   Curve Y.

     c.   Point C.

     d.   Point E.

     e.   Curve Z.

     f.   Curve X.

     g.   Point G.

     h.   Point H.

     i.   Firm One.

4.   a. $5, assuming there are no transactions costs or capacity constraints, and that
          consumers are informed about the prices charged by the firm. If either firm
          charged a price above $5, the other firm could slightly undercut the rival to steal
          all of its customers and increase its profits. Neither firm has an incentive to sell at
          a price below $5, since doing so would net it a loss. With both firms charging $5,

neither firm can enhance its profits by raising or lowering its price, and therefore $5 is the Bertrand equilibrium.

b. $5, since P = MC in a perfectly competitive market.

5.   a.   As Exhibit 9-5 below shows, Firm One's output falls.

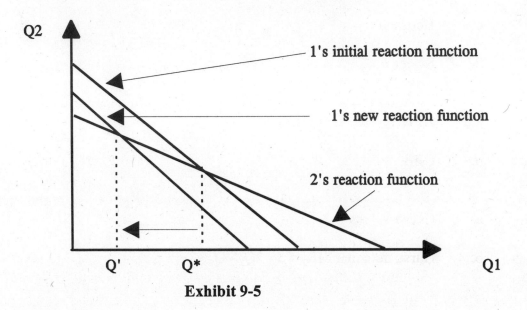

Exhibit 9-5

b.   As Exhibit 9-6 shows, a slight increase in Firm One's marginal cost has no impact on its output (or price). However, a large increase in Firm One's marginal cost would reduce it's output.

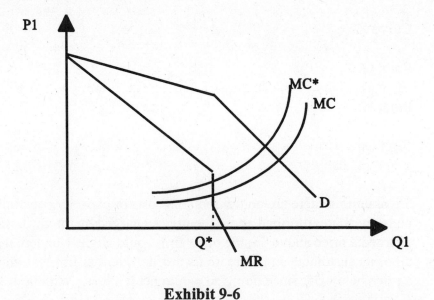

Exhibit 9-6

166

6. a. Yes, in the sense that it is the only firm in the market.

    b. The market for cleaning services is probably a contestable market. Therefore, Cleaning, Inc. must charge a price equal to marginal cost, or else potential entrants could quickly enter to earn profits. In other words, Cleaning, Inc. is disciplined by the threat of entry.

Answers to Technical Problems: Chapter 9

1. a. Yes; otherwise, it would make no sense to add up the two firm's outputs in the inverse market demand function.

    b. $MR_1 = 5 - 2Q_1 - Q_2$.

    c. Set $MR_1 = MC$ to get $5 - 2Q_1 - Q_2 = 1$. Solving this for Q_1 gives us Firm One's reaction function: $Q_1 = 2 - .5Q_2$.

    d. First, note that $MR_2 = 5 - 2Q_2 - Q_1$. Next, set $MR_2 = MC$ to get $5 - 2Q_2 - Q_1 = 1$. Solving this for Q_2 gives us Firm Two's reaction function: $Q_2 = 2 - .5Q_1$.

    e. $Q_1 = 4/3$, $Q_2 = 4/3$. To see this, plug Firm One's reaction function into Firm Two's to get $Q_1 = 2 - .5(2 - .5Q_1)$. Solving this for Q_1 gives $Q_1 = 4/3$. By symmetry, $Q_2 = 4/3$.

    f. $P = 2\ 1/3$. To see this, plug the equilibrium outputs into the inverse demand function to get $P = 5 - (4/3 + 4/3) = 2\ 1/3$.

2. a. $Q_1 = 2$. To see this, use the formula for Stackelberg output given in the text (and note that $c_1 = c_2 = \$1$, $a = 5$, and $b = 1$) to get $Q_1 = (5 + 1 - 2)/2 = 2$.

    b. $Q_2 = 1$. To see this, use the formula for Stackelberg output given in the text (and note that $c_1 = c_2 = \$1$, $a = 5$, $b = 1$, and $Q_1 = 2$) to get $Q_2 = (5 - 1)/2 - 2/2 = 1$.

    c. 3, since $Q_1 + Q_2 = 2 + 1 = 3$.

    d. $2, since $P = 5 - (2 + 1) = 2$.

3.   a.   P = $1, since P = MC = $1.

     b.   Q = 4. To see this set P = MC to get 5 - Q = 1, and solve for Q.

4.   a.   Q = 2. To see this, set MR = MC to get 5 - 2Q = 1 and solve to get Q = 2.

     b.   P = $3. To see this, note that P = 5 - Q = 5 - 2 = 3.

5.   Market output is highest under Bertrand, followed by Stackelberg, then Cournot, and finally collusion. Price is highest under collusion, followed by Cournot, then Stackelberg, and finally Bertrand.

Answers to Multiple Choice and True False Questions: Chapter 9

1.   b
2.   a
3.   d
4.   a
5.   d
6.   a
7.   e
8.   d
9.   a
10. a
11. False; view rival's price as constant
12. False; engage in quantity competition
13. False
14. True
15. False; quantities are set in both
16. True
17. False; P = MC in Bertrand
18. False; P = MC if the market is contestable
19. False; only the follower takes output as given
20. True

Chapter 10
Game Theory: Inside Oligopoly

Chapter 10 at a Glance

Key Concepts: Chapter 10

1. A strategy is a decision rule that describes the actions a player will take at each decision point.

2. The normal form representation of a game indicates the players of the game, the possible strategies of the players, and the payoffs to the players that result from alternative strategies.

3. A strategy is a dominant strategy if it results in the highest payoff regardless of the action of the opponent.

4. A strategy is secure if it guarantees the highest payoff, given the worst possible scenario.

5. A set of strategies constitute a Nash equilibrium if, given the strategies of the other players, no player can improve her payoff by unilaterally changing her strategy.

6. A one-shot game is a game that is played only once.

7. In a simultaneous-move game, players must make decisions without knowledge of the decisions made by other players.

8. In simultaneous-move one-shot games where a player has a dominant strategy, the optimal decision is to choose the dominant strategy.

9. In a one-shot simultaneous move bargaining game, the players have only one chance to reach an agreement, and the offers made in bargaining are made simultaneously.

10. In a repeated game, the underlying game is played more than one time.

11. An infinitely repeated game is a game that is played over and over again, forever. Players receive payoffs during each repetition of the game.

12. A trigger strategy is a strategy that is contingent on the past play of players in a game. A player adopting a trigger strategy continues to choose the same action until some player takes an action that "triggers" a different action by the player.

13. When the interest rate is low, firms in an infinitely repeated game can use trigger strategies to achieve collusive outcomes. If a player deviates from the "collusive strategy," he triggers punishments during future periods that last long enough to wipe out

the gains from having deviated from the collusive outcome. This threat of punishment can make collusion a Nash equilibrium in an infinitely repeated game.

14. Suppose a one-shot game is infinitely repeated, and the interest rate is i. Further, suppose the "cooperative" one-shot payoff to a player is π^{Coop}, the maximum one-shot payoff if the player cheats on the collusive outcome is π^{Cheat}, the one-shot Nash equilibrium payoff is π^N, and that

$$\frac{\pi^{Cheat} - \pi^{Coop}}{\pi^{Coop} - \pi^N} \leq \frac{1}{i}.$$

Then the cooperative (collusive) outcome can be sustained in the infinitely repeated game with the following trigger strategy:

Cooperate provided no player has ever cheated in the past. If any player cheats, "punish" the player by choosing the one-shot Nash equilibrium strategy forever after.

15. Finitely repeated games are games that are repeated a finite number of times; that is, games that eventually end.

16. There are two important classes of finitely repeated games: (1) games in which players do not know when the game will end; and (2) games in which players do know when the game will end.

17. When players know precisely when a repeated game will end, it leads to what is known as the end-of-period problem. In the final period there is no tomorrow, and there is no way to "punish" a player for doing something "wrong" in the last period. Consequently, in the last period, players will behave just like they would in a one-shot game. This leads to backwards unraveling, where the next to the last period is effectively the end of the game, and so on.

18. The extensive form of a game summarizes who the players are, information available to the players at each stage of the game, strategies available to the players, the order of the moves of the game, and the payoffs that result from the alternative strategies.

19. A set of strategies constitutes a subgame perfect equilibrium if (1) it is a Nash equilibrium, and (2) at each stage of the game (decision node) neither player can improve her payoff by changing her strategy.

20. In a two-stage sequential bargaining game, the first-mover in the bargaining game effectively makes a take-it-or-leave-it offer to the second-mover.

Questions: Chapter 10

1. Answer the following questions based on the one-shot simultaneous move game presented in Exhibit 10-1.

PLAYER B

Strategy	Left	Right
Up	1, 5	2, 4
Down	3, 6	4, 7

PLAYER A (to the left of the table)

Exhibit 10-1

a.   What is the secure strategy for player A?

b.   What is the secure strategy for player B?

c.   Does player A have a dominant strategy?

yes

d.   Does player B have a dominant strategy?

NO

e.   What are the Nash equilibrium strategies?

(D, R)

f.   What is the Nash equilibrium payoff for player A?

4

g.   What is the Nash equilibrium payoff for player B?

7

2. Answer the following questions based on the game in Exhibit 10-2:

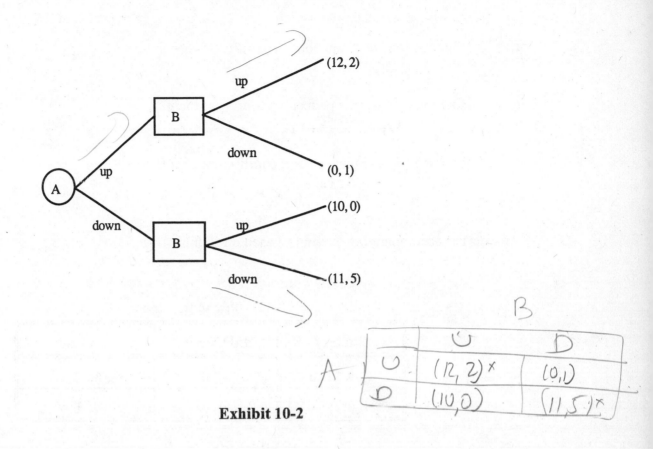

Exhibit 10-2

a. Is this a sequential-move or simultaneous-move game?

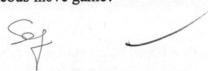

b. Which player moves first?

A

c. Give an example of a strategy for player A.

U or D

d.   Give an example of a strategy for player B.

        up↓up

e.   How many Nash equilibria are there?

        2   1D

f.   What are the Nash equilibrium payoffs?

        (11,5)

g.   How many subgame perfect equilibria are there?

        (up , up↓up)
              d↓d

h.   What are the subgame perfect equilibrium payoffs?

        (11,5) (12,2)

3.   Answer the accompanying questions based on Exhibit 10-3.

                                    FIRM B

	Strategy	Low Price	High Price
FIRM A	Low Price	0, 0	5, -1
	High Price	-1, 5	1, 1

                            Exhibit 10-3

a.   What oligopoly situation does this game represent?

        Bertrand

b.   Suppose this is a one-shot game, and Firm A agreed to charge a high price. What
      is Firm B's best response?

        Low

c.   What are the Nash equilibrium profits to the one-shot game?

        (0,0)

4. Suppose the game in Exhibit 10-4 is repeated 2 times. Each firm agrees to charge a high price, provided the rival has never charged a low price in any previous period. If its rival deviates from this plan, a firm will revert to charging a low price thereafter. The interest rate is zero.

FIRM B

	Strategy	Low Price	High Price
FIRM A	Low Price	0, 0	5, -1
	High Price	-1, 5	3, 3

Exhibit 10-4

a. Assuming Firm B lives up to the agreement, what will Firm A earn if it lives up to the agreement?

b. Assuming Firm B lives up to the agreement, what will Firm A earn if it deviates from the agreement in the first period?

c. Assuming Firm B lives up to the agreement, what will Firm A earn if it deviates from the agreement in the second period?

d. Does the agreement provide a means of sustaining the collusive outcome (that is, charging high prices in both periods)?

5. Now suppose the game in Exhibit 10-4 is infinitely repeated. Each firm agrees to charge a high price, provided the rival has never charged a low price in any previous period. If its rival deviates from this plan, a firm will revert to charging a low price forever after. The interest rate is 50 percent.

a. Assuming Firm B lives up to the agreement, what will Firm A earn if it lives up to the agreement?

b. Assuming Firm B lives up to the agreement, what will Firm A earn if it deviates from the agreement?

c. Does the agreement provide a means of sustaining the collusive outcome (that is, charging high prices in both periods)?

d. Would your answer change if the interest rate was 100 percent?

Technical Problems: Chapter 10

1. Natalie and Mitchell found 2 coins on the playground, and after further inspection, realized they were both quarters. After a short squabble, their mom informed them that they had to independently write down how many coins they wanted. If the total number of coins Mitch and Natalie asked for equaled 2 coins, then they could each keep the amount they wrote down. Otherwise, Mom would remove 1 quarter from each of their piggy banks.

   a. Write down this game in normal form.

b.   What are the Nash equilibria to the game?

2.   Consider the situation in problem 1, but now suppose Mom lets Natalie make Mitchell an offer to give him 0, 1, or 2 quarters. Mitchell can either "accept" or "reject" Natalie's offer. However, if they are unable to reach an agreement (that is, Mitchell reject's Natalie's offer), Mom will remove 1 quarter from each of their piggy banks.

a.   Write down this game in extensive form.

b.   What is the subgame perfect outcome of the game?

3. Your firm must decide whether or not to introduce a new product. If you introduce the new product, your rival will have to decide whether to clone the new product, or not. If you don't introduce the new product, you and your rival will earn $10 million each. If you do introduce the new product, and your rival clones it, you will lose $5 million and your rival will earn $20 million. If you introduce the new product and your rival does not clone it, you will make $5 million and your rival will make $0.

a. Write this game in extensive form.

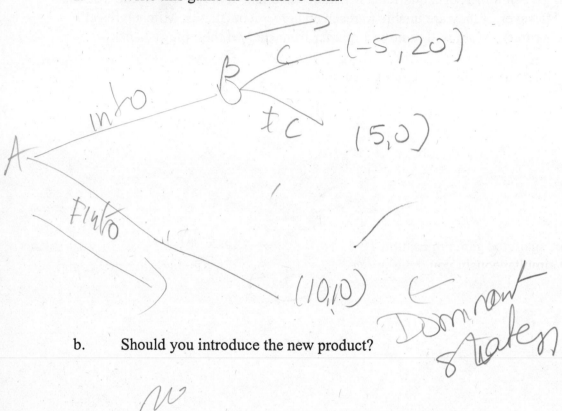

b. Should you introduce the new product?

4. Consider the one-shot, simultaneous move game in Exhibit 10-5, and answer the accompanying questions:

FIRM B

	Strategy	Y	Z
FIRM A	W	5, 5	0, 0
	X	0, 0	3, 3

Exhibit 10-5

178

a.   Suppose Firm B plays Y. What is Firm A's best response?

b.   Suppose Firm A plays W. What is Firm B's best response?

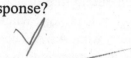

c.   Does firm A have a dominant strategy?

No

d.   What are the Nash equilibria to this game?

e.   What is this type of game called?

5.   Consider again the game in Exhibit 10-5. Now suppose you are Firm A, and instead of moving simultaneously you get to move first. Firm B gets to observe your move, and then make its play.

a.   What strategy would you choose, and why?

b.   Would Firm B object to your getting the first move? Explain.

6. ACME and AAA compete in a duopoly by producing and selling special titanium plated carriage bolts. The two firms use labor, materials and machines to produce virtually identical bolts. Due to technological constraints, ACME can produce only 200 or 300 bolts, but AAA can produce either 200, 300, or 400 bolts. As the manager of ACME, you must decide how much output to produce in order to maximize profits. ACME's cost function is given by $C_{ACME} = 15Q_{ACME}$, where $15Q_{ACME}$ represents direct variable costs of production. You have no idea what AAA's costs are, but your marketing department has provided you with the following information about the market demand for bolts:

Combined Output of ACME and AAA	Price of Bolts
400 bolts	$22
500 bolts	$20
600 bolts	$20
700 bolts	$20

a. Write the game in normal form.

b. If ACME has a first-mover advantage and can commit to an output before AAA, what number of bolts should it produce?

180

Multiple Choice and True/False Questions: Chapter 10

1. Which of the following conditions is necessary for a subgame perfect Nash equilibrium?
   a. The existence of dominant strategies for both players.
   b. The existence of a dominant strategy for one player and the existence of secure strategy for another player.
   c. All threats must be credible.
   d. none of the above

2. Which of the following is not true for a Nash equilibrium of two-player simultaneous move games?
   a. The joint payoffs of the two players might be lower than the joint payoffs that arise under some other set of strategies.
   b. Given the other player's strategy stipulated in that Nash equilibrium, a player can improve his payoff by changing his strategy.
   c. A Nash equilibrium, if it exists, is unique.
   d. b. and c.

3. Which of the following is true?
   a. A Nash equilibrium is always subgame perfect.
   b. A subgame perfect equilibrium is always a Nash equilibrium.
   c. A Nash equilibrium is always subgame perfect in a multistage game.
   d. Subgame perfect equilibrium and Nash equilibrium are the same concept only applied to sequential and simultaneous move games, respectively.

4. A Nash equilibrium with a non credible threat as a component is:
   a. a secure equilibrium
   b. a perfect equilibrium
   c. a sequential equilibrium
   d. none of the above.

5. It is more difficult to sustain tacit collusion in an infinitely repeated game if:
   a. the present value of cheating is higher.
   b. there are more players in the game.
   c. the interest rate is higher
   d. all of the above

6. Which of the following is true?
   a. An extensive form representation usually provides more information than the normal form representation of a game.
   b. A normal form game is most useful for sequential-move games.
   c. All of the above are true.

d. None of the above are true.

7. Game theory suggests that, when there is not repeated interaction, Bertrand duopolists
   a. will charge prices higher than marginal cost.
   b. will be able to collude.
   c. All of the above.
   d. None of the above

Answer questions 8, 9, and 10 based on the following information: If you advertise and your rival advertises, you each will earn $0 million in profits. If neither of you advertise, you will each earn $1 million in profits. However, if one of you advertises and the other does not, the firm that advertises will earn $10 million and the non advertising firm will lose $1 million.

8. Which of the following is true?
   a. A dominant strategy for Firm A is to advertise.
   b. A dominant strategy for Firm B is to advertise.
   c. A Nash equilibrium is for both firms to advertise.
   d. All of the above are true

9. What are the Nash equilibrium payoffs for the firms in a one-shot game?
   a. (0, 0)
   b. (0, 10)
   c. (10, 0)
   d. The game does not have a Nash equilibrium.

10. Which of the following is true?
   a. A secure strategy for Firm A is to not advertise.
   b. A secure strategy for Firm A is to advertise.
   c. All of the above are true.
   d. None of the above are true.

11. True or False: In a one-shot game, a collusive strategy always represents a Nash equilibrium.

12. True or False: A secure strategy occurs when each player is doing the best he can regardless of what the other player is doing.

13. True or False: In a two player simultaneous move game, if both players have a dominant strategy, then the situation where the two players play their dominant strategy comprises a Nash equilibrium.

14. True or False: Every perfect equilibrium is a Nash equilibrium.

182

15. True or False: In an infinitely repeated game, collusion is always a Nash equilibrium.

16. True or False: In a finitely repeated game with a certain end period, collusion is generally not feasible during the last period because effective punishments cannot be used thereafter.

17. True or False: In an infinitely repeated game with a low interest rate, collusion is unlikely because the game unravels so that effective punishment cannot be used during any time period.

18. True or False: A dominant strategy is the optimal strategy for a player no matter what the opponent does.

19. True or False: Collusion is more likely in industries with a large number of firms.

20. True or False: Coordination games have multiple Nash equilibria.

Answers to Questions: Chapter 10

1. a. Down. The worst that can happen by playing up is to earn 1, while the worst that can happen by playing down is to earn 3.

    b. Left. The worst that can happen by playing right is to earn 4, while the worst that can happen by playing left is to earn 5.

    c. Yes. Playing down pays more, regardless of what the opponent does.

    d. No. Playing Left is best against up; playing right is best against down.

    e. (Down, Right). Neither player can gain by unilaterally deviating from their strategy, given what the other is playing.

    f. 4

    g. 7

2. a. Sequential-move game.

b. Player A.

c. Up. Notice that player A's strategies cannot depend on what B does, since A moves first.

d. Up if A plays up, down if A plays down. Notice that the second player can take into account what A did when formulating her strategy.

e. 2. One involves A playing up and B playing up. The other is for B to threaten to play down if A plays up, and therefore for A to play down and B to play down.

f. (12, 2) and (11, 5)

g. 1. The (11, 5) equilibrium is not subgame perfect because the reason A plays down in this equilibrium is the threat by B to play down if A plays up. But if A plays up, it is not in B's best interest to play down, but rather to play up.

h. (12, 2)

3. a. Bertrand oligopoly.

b. Low price, since 5 > 1.

c. (0, 0)

4. a. 6. It earns 3 in the first period, and 3 in the second period.

b. 5. It will earn 5 the first period, but this will trigger a low price by the rival which means 0 will be earned the second period.

c. 8. It will earn 3 the first period (when it cooperates), and 5 during the second period when it deviates from the agreement by charging a low price.

d. No. We just showed that firm A would want to deviate during period 2.

5. a. $3 + (1.5)^{-1} \times 3 + (1.5)^{-2} \times 3 \ldots = 3(1 + .5)/.5 = 9$.

b. 5. It earns 5 the first period it deviates, and zero thereafter.

c. Yes; the present value of the gains to cooperating (9) exceed the gains from deviating (5), so it pays to cooperate.

d.   Cooperation still works, since $PV_{cheat} = 5 < PV_{coop} = 3(1+1)/1 = 6$.

Answers to Technical Problems: Chapter 10

1.   a.   The normal form game is shown in Exhibit 10-6:

Mitchell

	Strategy	0	1	2
Natalie	0	-.25 , -.25	-.25 , -.25	0 , .50
	1	-.25 , -.25	.25 , .25	-.25 , -.25
	2	.50 , 0	-.25 , -.25	-.25 , -.25

Exhibit 10-6

b.   There are three Nash equilibria: one where Natalie gets 2 coins and Mitchell gets none; one where Natalie gets 0 coins and Mitchell 2; and one where each gets one coin.

2.   a.   The extensive form is shown in Exhibit 10-7.

b.   Natalie gets 2 quarters, Mitchell gets none. Natalie makes a take-it or leave it offer, and given the payoffs, Mitchell has no incentive to refuse (if you think he might want to refuse to spite his sister, then your payoffs should be different in your extensive form game).

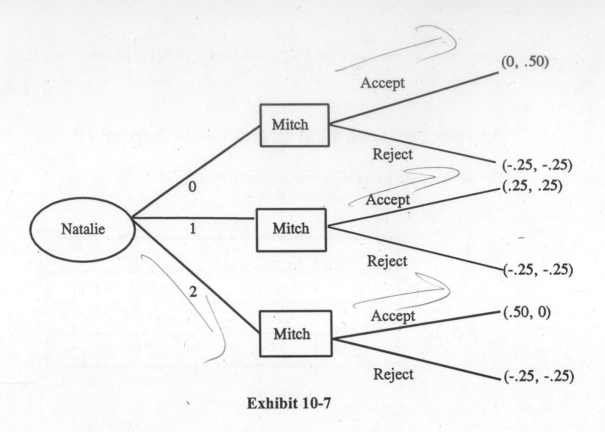

Exhibit 10-7

3. a. The extensive form is shown in Exhibit 10-8.

    b. No. In fact, regardless of what your opponent will do, your best strategy is to not introduce. Stated differently, not introducing the new product is a dominant strategy in this sequential move game.

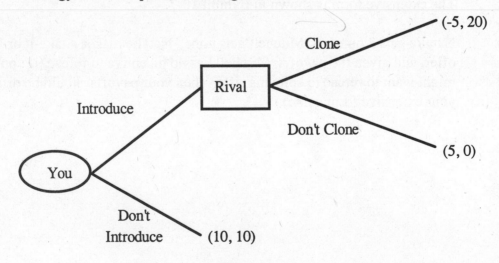

Exhibit 10-8

4. a. W.

b. Y.

c. No; A's best strategy depends on what B does.

d. (W, Y) and (X, Z)

e. A coordination game.

5. a. W. Once B observed this move, his best response would be Y, and both players earn payoffs of 5.

b. No. If B moved first, he would choose Y, in which case A would see this and choose W. In this case, each player still earns 5. Moving sequentially can solve the coordination problem.

6. a. The normal form game is shown in Exhibit 10-9. Note that we cannot compute AAA's payoffs since we do not know what their costs are. To compute ACME's payoffs, note that if both firms produce 200 units, total market output is 400 units and price will be $22. Since ACME's unit costs are $15, under this scenario ACME contributes $7 toward the bottom line for each unit sold. Thus, ACME's payoff is $7 x 200 = $1400 if each firm produces 200 units. Next, note that any other combination of outputs by the two firms leads to a market price of $20 per unit, which means in these scenarios ACME contributes $5 toward its bottom line for each unit sold. Thus if ACME produces 200 units and AAA produces either 300 or 400 units, ACME earns a payoff of $5 x 200 = $1,000. If ACME produces 300 units, it earns a payoff of $5 x 300 =$1500 if AAA produces 200, 300, or 400 units.

		AAA		
	Strategy	200	300	400
ACME	200	$1400 , $?	$1000 , $?	$1000 , $?
	300	$1500 , $?	$1500 , $?	$1500 , $?

Exhibit 10-9

b.   ACME's dominant strategy is to produce 300 units – regardless of what AAA does, earns a payoff of $1500 by producing 300 units, and this exceeds what could be earned by producing 200 units. This means that regardless of whether ACME moves first, second, or at the same time as AAA, ACME's optimal strategy is to produce 300 units. This is true even though we don't know AAA's costs or payoffs!

Answers to Multiple Choice and True/False Questions:
Chapter 10

1.   c
2.   d
3.   b
4.   d
5.   d
6.   a
7.   d
8.   d
9.   a
10.   b
11.   False
12.   False; this is a dominant strategy
13.   True
14.   True
15.   False; only if the interest rate is low enough
16.   True
17.   False
18.   True
19.   False; less likely
20.   True

Chapter 11
Pricing Strategies for Firms with Market Power

Chapter 11 at a Glance

Key Concepts: Chapter 11

1. The price that maximizes profit is given by

$$P = \left[\frac{E_F}{1 + E_F} \right] x \ MC,$$

where E_F is the own price elasticity of demand for the firm's product, and MC is the firm's marginal cost. The term in brackets is the optimal markup factor.

2. If there are N identical firms in a Cournot oligopoly, then the profit-maximizing price is

$$P = \left[\frac{N \ E_M}{1 + N \ E_M} \right] x \ MC,$$

where N is the number of firms in the industry, E_M is the market elasticity of demand, and MC is marginal cost.

3. Price discrimination refers to charging different groups of consumers different prices.

4. First-degree price discrimination refers to the practice of charging each consumer the maximum price he or she would be willing to pay for each unit of the good purchased. By adopting this strategy, a firm extracts all surplus from consumers, and thus earns the highest possible profits.

5. Second-degree price discrimination is the practice of posting a discrete schedule of declining prices for different ranges of quantities.

6. Third-degree price discrimination is the practice of charging different groups of consumers different prices for the same product.

7. If the following conditions are satisfied, a firm can enhance profits by engaging in third degree price discrimination:

   a. Consumers are partitioned into two types, with one type having a more elastic demand than the other.

   b. The firm has a means of identifying consumer types.

c. There is no resale market for the good.

8. In order to maximize profits, a third-degree price discriminating firm with market power produces the output where the marginal revenue to each group equals marginal cost:

$$\underbrace{P_1 \left[\frac{1 + E_1}{E_1} \right]}_{MR_1} = MC$$

$$\underbrace{P_2 \left[\frac{1 + E_2}{E_2} \right]}_{MR_2} = MC.$$

9. A firm can enhance profits by engaging in two-part pricing: charge a per unit price that equals marginal cost, and in addition, charge a fixed-fee equal to the consumer surplus each consumer would receive at this per-unit price.

10. By packaging units of a product together and selling them in one block, the firm earns more than by posting a simple per-unit price. The profit-maximizing price on a package is the total value the consumer receives for the package, including consumer's surplus.

11. Commodity bundling is the practice of bundling several different products together, and selling them at a single "bundle price."

12. When a firm faces capacity constraints and demand is higher at some times of the day than at others, a firm may enhance profits by peak-load pricing: charge a higher price during peak times than is charged during off-peak times.

13. Whenever the demand for two products produced by a firm are inter-related through costs or demand, a firm may enhance profits by cross subsidization: selling one product at or below cost, and the other product at a price above cost.

14. A firm that uses a price matching strategy advertises a price, and a promise to "match" any lower price offered by a competitor. Such strategies lead to higher prices.

15. Double marginalization occurs when an upstream and downstream division within a firm both mark up prices in excess of marginal cost. The result is less than optimal overall firm profits.

16. Optimal transfer pricing refers to the internal price at which an upstream division should sell inputs to the firm's downstream division in order to maximize the overall profits of the firm.

17. Suppose the downstream division has a marginal cost of assembling the final output, denoted MC_d, that is in addition to cost of acquiring the input from the upstream division. Then the overall profits of the firm are maximized when the upstream division produces engines such that it's marginal cost, MC_u, equals the net marginal revenue to the downstream division (NMR_d):

$$NMR_d = MR_d - MC_d = MC_u.$$

This determines an optimal output, denoted Q^*. The optimal transfer price, P_T, equals the upstream division's marginal cost of producing the aomount of input required by the downstream division to produce Q^* units of final output.

Questions: Chapter 11

1. Use Exhibit 11-1, which shows demand conditions for a firm with market power, to answer the following questions.

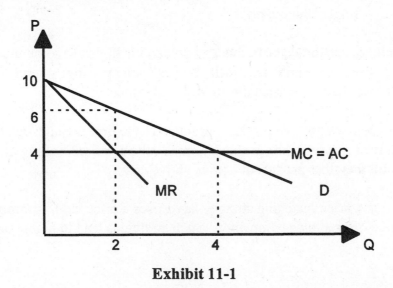

Exhibit 11-1

a. Suppose the firm charges a per unit price to consumers. What price maximizes profits?

$6

b. If the firm charges a per unit price to consumers, what will be the firm's output?

2

c. If the firm charges a per unit price to consumers, what will be the firm's profit?

$$12 - \frac{4}{x}(2 = 4$$

2. Now suppose the firm in Exhibit 11-1 can engage in two-part pricing.

a. What is the optimal fixed fee?

$$\frac{6 \times 4}{2} = 12$$

b. What is the optimal per unit price?

4

c. What are the firm's profits?

12

3. Now suppose the firm in Exhibit 11-1 decides to package 2 units of the product together, and sell them as a block.

   a. What is the optimal price to charge for a block of 2 units?

   b. What are the firm's profits if it packages 2 units for sale?

4. Determine the type of pricing strategy that will maximize profits in each of the following situations:

   a. A firm's demand is very low on weekends, but quite high during the week.

   Peak load

   b. A firm knows that students have a much more elastic demand for their product than do senior citizens.

   3rd PX

   c. Consumers have significantly different preferences for different stereo components. Some are willing to pay handily for tape players but not for CD players, while others will pay handily for CD players but not tape players.

   Bundle

5. List three strategies that can be used by firms to enhance profits in an environment of extreme price competition.

a.

b.

c.

Technical Problems: Chapter 11

1. The manager of a supermarket competes in a monopolistically competitive market, and buys canned goods from a supplier at a price of $.25 per can. The manager hired an econometrician, who estimated the elasticity of demand for canned goods at her store to be -2. What price should the manager charge for can of green beans in order to maximize profits?

$$MC = .25 \qquad E = -2$$

$$MC = P\left(\frac{1+E}{E}\right)$$

$$MC \frac{E}{1+E} = P$$

$$.25\left(\frac{-2}{-1}\right) = P = \$.5 .$$

2. Four firms compete in a homogeneous product Cournot industry. The market elasticity of demand for the product is -0.5, and each firm's marginal cost of production is $2. What is the profit-maximizing equilibrium price?

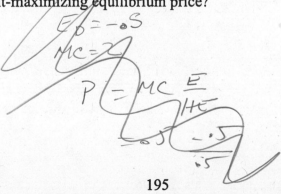

$$E_D = -.5$$
$$MC = 2$$
$$P = MC \frac{E}{1+E}$$
$$-.5$$
$$.5$$

3. You are the manager of the only janitorial service in town. The population in your town consists of yuppies and older retired families. Yuppies live on Highlife Street, while retired folks live on Beat Street. A friend of yours is an econometrician, and as a favor she performed an econometric analysis of your situation and found that yuppies have an elasticity of demand for cleaning services of -3, while retired folks have an elasticity of demand of -5.

$E_y = -3$

$E_R = -5$

a. An intuitive level, do your friend's estimates of the elasticities seem reasonable?

yes

b. If it costs you $15 for each hour you spend cleaning a house, what hourly rate should you charge yuppies to maximize profits?

$C = 15$

$$MR = P\left(1 + \frac{E}{E}\right)$$

$$MC = P\left(1 + \frac{E}{E}\right)$$

$$MC\left(\frac{E}{1+E}\right) = P$$

$$Y: \quad 15\left(\frac{-3}{1-3}\right) = P = 22.5$$

c. If it costs you $15 for each hour you spend cleaning a house, what hourly rate should you charge retirees to maximize profits?

1

4.   Suppose an individual sports enthusiast's monthly inverse demand for a health spa is

$$P = 30 - Q.$$

The marginal cost to the firm of each visit is \$0, but the firm has fixed costs of \$4,500 per month.

a.   Sketch the demand curve in Exhibit 11-2.

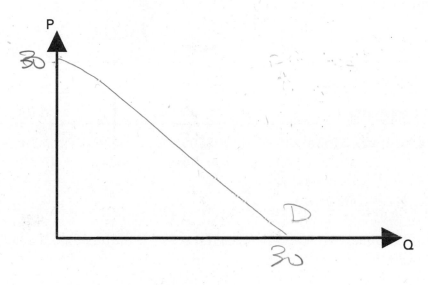

Exhibit 11-2

b.   What is the optimal pricing strategy for the firm to charge this sports enthusiast for a membership?

$$\frac{30 \times 30}{2} = 450$$

c.   How many memberships would the firm have to sell in order to turn a profit?

10

197

d.   How many days per month will the typical sport's enthusiast visit the spa?

30 days

5.   Suppose three purchasers of a stereo system have the following valuations for components:

	CD Player	Tape Player
Consumer One	$200	$300
Consumer Two	$300	$200
Consumer Three	$500	$0

The firm's costs are zero.

a.   How much will the firm make if it sells CD players for $200 and tape players for $200?

600 + 400 = 1000

b.   How much will the firm make if it sells CD players for $400 and tape players for $300?

400 + 300 = 700

c. How much will the firm make if it packages CD players and tape players together and sells the bundle for $500?

1500

d. If the manager knows the valuations and identity of each consumer, what is the optimal pricing strategy?

800

6. Starway specializes in manufacturing high-performance automobiles. Each of the firm's cars contain a unique engine that is produced at the firm's European plant at a cost of $C_u(Q_e) = Q_e^2$. Once produced, the engines are shipped exclusively to the firm's Asian plant, where the cars are assembled shipped to the market at a cost of $C_D(Q) = 100 Q$. The demand for the firm's cars is given $P = 500 - Q$.

a. Determine Starway's optimal output.

b Determine Starway's optimal price for cars.

c. Explain how the firm can induce plant managers to produce the required number of engines and cars.

Multiple Choice and True/False Questions: Chapter 11

 1. You are the manager of a store that can buy milk from a supplier at $3.00 per gallon. If you believe the elasticity of demand for milk by customers at your store is constant and equal to -1, then your revenue maximizing price is

a. 2.00 $MC = 3$
b. 2.50 $E = -1$
c. 4.00
d. all of the above.

2. A monopoly produces a good at marginal cost of $1 per unit and faces a demand elasticity of -2. What price should it charge to optimize it profits?

a. $1 per unit $MC = 1$
b. $2 per unit $E = -2$
c. $3 per unit
d. $4 per unit

$MC = P\left(\frac{1+E}{E}\right)$

$1 = P\left(\frac{1-2}{-2}\right)$

3. A monopoly produces at a marginal cost of $10 per unit. It faces an inverse demand function given by P = 60 - Q. Which of the following is the marginal revenue function for the firm?

a. MR = 60 - 2Q. $MC = 10$
b. MR = 30 - Q. $P = 60 - Q$
c. MR = 120 - Q. $MR = 60 - 2Q$
d. MR = 60 - 0.5Q.

4. Which of the following pricing strategies can enhance the profits of firms with market power?
    a. commodity bundling
    b. price discrimination
    c. two-part pricing
    d. all of the above

5. Which of the following statements is false?
    a. The more elastic the demand, the higher is the profit-maximizing markup.
    b. The more elastic the demand, the lower is the profit-maximizing markup.
    c. The higher the marginal cost, the higher the profit-maximizing price.
    d. The higher the average cost, other things equal, the lower are profits.

$$MR = P\left(\frac{1+E}{E}\right)$$

6. The idea of charging the same consumer a fixed fee as well as a fee for each unit purchased is called:
    a. price discrimination.
    b. two-part pricing.
    c. price matching.
    d. none of the above.

7. Which of the following conditions are required in order for third-degree price discrimination to be an effective way of enhancing firm profits: 3
    a. ability to identify consumer types.
    b. ability to resell the good.
    c. identical demand elasticities.
    d. all of the above

8. The most a consumer will pay for a block of 4 season tickets is $100. If faced with a single ticket price of $25, the consumer would buy 2 tickets. To maximize revenues, what price should a firm charge the consumer for a block of 4 tickets?
    a. $25
    b. $50
    c. $75
    d. $100

9. What should a firm charge for a package of three t-shirts if a typical consumer's inverse demand function is P = 10 - Q?
    a. $7
    b. $21
    c. $21.50
    d. $25.50

201

10. A campus auditorium sells weekend tickets at a higher price than during the week. This is an example of:
   a. commodity bundling
   b. peak-load pricing.
   c. price matching
   d. randomized pricing.

11. True or False: Two part pricing is useful for enhancing profits in a homogeneous product Bertrand duopoly.

12. True or false: Price matching strategies may fail to enhance profits when firms have different marginal costs.

13. True or False: Two part pricing results in consumers receiving no consumer surplus.

14. True or False: The purpose of randomized pricing is to reduce the information consumers and competitors have about your price.

15. True or False: If a monopolist must charge a single price to all consumers, and if the elasticity of demand at that price and quantity is -0.5, then the monopolist is producing too much output.

16. True or False: A third-degree price discriminating monopolist maximizes profits by charging a higher price to the group with the most inelastic demand.

17. True or False: Two-part pricing eliminates the deadweight loss than can arise under monopoly.

18. True or False: Price matching strategies generally result in lower prices for consumers.

19. True or False: Peak load pricing is typically used in situations when the firm faces a capacity constraint and faces demand fluctuations at different times of the day or week.

20. True or False: If each divisional manager maximizes divisional profits, then the firm's overall profits are also maximized.

202

Answers to Questions: Chapter 11

1.   a. $6. MR = MC at 2 units of output, so the profit maximizing price is $6.

      b.   2 units. This output is where MR = MC.

      c. $4. This is computed as ($6 - $4) x 2 = $4.

2.   a. $12. The optimal fixed fee is equal to the would-be consumer surplus at the point where P = MC. P = MC at 4 units of output, so the corresponding consumer surplus is .5 x ($10 - $4) x 4 = $12.

      b. $4. The optimal per unit price is marginal cost, which ensures that consumers buy 4 units.

      c. $12. All profits come from the fixed fee.

3.   a. $16. This is computed as the rectangle with area ($6 - 0) x 2 = $12, plus the consumer surplus triangle which has area .5 x ($10 - $6) x 2 = $4.

      b. $8. The cost to the firm of producing 2 units is AC x Q = $4 x 2 = $8. This must be subtracted from the revenues computed in part a.

4.   a.   Peak-load pricing.

      b.   Price discrimination.

      c.   Commodity bundling.

5.   a.   Price matching.

      b.   Randomized pricing.

      c.   Introducing brand loyalty.

Answers to Technical Problems: Chapter 11

1. 50 cents. Using the markup formula, $P = MC \times E_F/(1 + E_F) = .25 \times -2/(1 - 2) = \$0.5$.

2. $4. Using the markup formula for Cournot oligopoly, $P = MC \times N\, E_M/(1 + N\, E_M) = \$2 \times (4)(-.5)/(1 + (4)(-.5)) = \$2 \times (-2)/(1 - 2) = \$4$.

3. a. Yes, they do seem reasonable. One would expect retired people to have lower opportunity cost than yuppies, and therefore have a more elastic demand for janitorial services.

   b. $22.50. This is computed as $P = MC \times E_Y/(1 + E_Y) = \$15 \times -3/(1 - 3) = \$15 \times 3/2 = \$22.50$.

   c. $18.75. This is computed as $P = MC \times E_R/(1 + E_R) = \$15 \times -5/(1 - 5) = \$15 \times 5/4 = \$18.75$.

4. a. Your graph should look like the one in Exhibit 11-3.

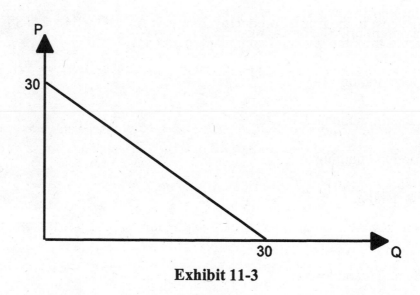

Exhibit 11-3

   b. Charge a fixed fee of $450 per month for a membership, and then let the customer come in for free each time he or she visits. To see this, notice that consumers surplus is maximized when Q = 30. Consumer surplus is therefore .5 x ($30 - 0) x 30 = $450, and this is the optimal fixed fee.

c. Each consumer nets the firm $450 in revenues. To cover the $4,500 fixed costs, 10 customers would have to join. Any customers in excess of 10 would lead to profits.

d. At a zero price per visit, each customer would visit the spa 30 times each month, or about once a day.

5. a. $1,000. All consumers are willing to pay at least $200 for a CD player, so all three consumers will buy one to net the firm 3 x $200 = $600 in CD sales. Only consumers 1 and 2 are willing to pay $200 for a tape player, so the firm will net 2 x $200 = $400 in tape player sales. Therefore, the firm would make $1,000 in total sales.

    b. $700. Only consumer three would buy a CD player for $400, while only consumer one would buy a tape player for $300? Total profits are therefore $300 + $400 = $700.

    c. $1,500. Notice that the value of a CD player and a tape player is $200 + $300 = $500 for consumer one, $300 + $200 = $500 for consumer two, and $500 + 0 = $500 for consumer three. Therefore, all three consumers would buy the bundle, netting the firm 3 x $500 = $1,500.

    d. Charge $500 for a bundle containing a CD player and a tape player. This commodity bundling scheme nets profits to the firm are the same as if it charged each consumer the maximum price he or she would pay for each component separately.

6. a. Assuming each car has one engine ($Q_e = Q$), the number of engines that maximizes overall firm profits is determined by setting the $NMR_D = MC_U$:
$$NMR_D = 500 - 2Q_e - 100 = 2Q_e.$$
Solving for Q_e, the European plant should produce $Q_e = 100$ engines, and (since $Q = Q_e$) the Asian plant should produce 100 cars.

    b. The optimal price for the firm's cars, therefore, is $P = 500 - 100 = 400$.

    c. The firm can achieve this outcome by setting the optimal transfer price at the European plant's marginal cost of producing 100 engines, or $P_T = \$200$, and by then providing divisional managers an incentive to maximize their plant's profits given this transfer price.

Answers to Multiple Choice and True/False Questions:
Chapter 11

1. d
2. b
3. a
4. d
5. a
6. b
7. a
8. d
9. d
10. b
11. False
12. True
13. True
14. True
15. True
16. True
17. True
18. False; higher prices
19. True
20. False

Chapter 12
The Economics of Information

Chapter 12 at a Glance

Key Concepts: Chapter 12

1. The mean (or expected value) of a random variable, x, is defined as the sum of the probabilities different outcomes occur times the resulting outcomes. Formally, if the possible outcomes of the random variable are x_1, x_2,..., x_n, and the corresponding probabilities of the outcomes are q_1, q_2,..., q_n, then the expected value of x is given by

$$Ex = q_1x_1 + q_2x_2 + ... + q_nx_n,$$

where $q_1 + q_2 + ... + q_n = 1$.

2. The variance of a random variable is defined as the sum of the probabilities different outcomes occur times the squared deviations from the mean of the random variable. Formally, if the possible outcomes of the random variable are x_1, x_2,..., x_n, their corresponding probabilities are q_1, q_2,..., q_n, and the expected value of x is given by Ex, then the variance of x is given by

$$\sigma^2 = q_1(x_1 - Ex)^2 + q_2(x_2 - Ex)^2 + ... + q_n(x_n - Ex)^2.$$

The standard deviation is simply the square root of the variance:

$$\sigma = \sqrt{\sigma^2} = \sqrt{q_1(x_1 - Ex)^2 + q_2(x_2 - Ex)^2 + ... + q_n(x_n - Ex)^2}.$$

3. A risk averse person prefers a sure amount of $M to a risky prospect with an expected value of $M.

4. A risk loving individual prefers a risky prospect with an expected value of $M to a sure amount of $M.

5. A risk neutral individual is indifferent between a risky prospect with an expected value of $M, and a certain amount of $M.

6. The reservation price, R, is the price such that the consumer is indifferent between purchasing at that price and searching for a lower price. Formally, if EB(p) is the expected benefit of searching for a price lower than p, and c represents the cost per search, the reservation price satisfies

$$EB(R) = c.$$

7. The optimal search rule is such that the consumer rejects prices above the reservation price (R), and accepts prices below the reservation price. Stated differently, the optimal

search strategy is to search for a better price when the price charged by a store is above the reservation price, and stop searching when a price below the reservation price is found.

8. Asymmetric information exists whenever some people have better information than others.

9. Adverse selection generally arises when an individual has hidden characteristics -- characteristics that it knows, but that are unknown by the other party in an economic transaction. Adverse selection results when a selection process generates a pool of individuals with undesirable characteristics.

10. Moral hazard generally occurs when one party takes hidden actions -- actions that it knows another party cannot observe -- that harm another party in a transaction. It is most prevalent in situations where a contract insulates one party from loss. In these instances, the insured party often takes hidden actions that harms the other party in the contract.

11. Signaling occurs when an informed party sends a signal (or indicator) of his or her hidden characteristics to an uninformed party, in an attempt to provide information about these hidden characteristics.

12. Screening occurs when an uninformed party attempts to sort individuals according to their characteristics. This sorting may be achieved through a *self-selection device*: individuals who have information about their own characteristics are presented with a set of options, and the options they choose reveals their characteristics to the uninformed party.

13. Managers and other market participants can use signaling and screening to mitigate some of the problems that arise when one party to a transaction has hidden characteristics.

14. An English auction is an ascending sequential bid auction, where bidders observe the bids of others and determine whether they wish to increase the bid. The auction ends when a single bidder is left, at which point this bidder obtains the item and pays the auctioneer the amount of his bid.

15. A first-price sealed bid auction is a simultaneous move auction, where bidders simultaneously submit bids on a piece of paper. The auctioneer awards the item to the high bidder, who pays the amount he bid.

16. A second-price sealed bid auction is a simultaneous move auction, where bidders simultaneously submit bids. The auctioneer awards the item to the high bidder, who pays the amount bid by the second-highest bidder.

17. A Dutch auction is a descending sequential bid auction. The auctioneer begins with a high asking price, and gradually reduces the asking price until one of the bidders announces she is willing to pay that price for the item.

18. The Dutch and first price sealed bid auctions are strategically equivalent. That is, the optimal bids by participants are identical for both auctions.

19. Independent private values refers to an auction environment in which each bidder knows his own valuation of the item but does not know other bidders' valuations, and in which each bidder's valuation does not depend on other bidders' valuations of the object.

20. An auction environment with affiliated (or correlated) value estimates is one in which (a) bidders do not know their own valuation of the item or the valuations of others, (b) each bidder uses his or her own information to estimate their valuation, and (c) these value estimates are affiliated.

21. Affiliated value estimates means that a higher value estimate by one bidder makes it more likely that other bidders also have high value estimates.

22. A common values auction environment refers to a situation where the true value of the item is the same for all bidders, but this common value is unknown. Bidders each use their own (private) information to form an estimate of the item's true common value.

23. In a common-values auction, the winner is the bidder who is the most optimistic about the true value of the item. To avoid the winner's curse, a bidder should revise downward his or her private estimate of the value to account for this fact.

24. A player's optimal bidding strategy in an English auction with independent, private valuations is to remain active until the price exceeds his or her own valuation of the object.

25. In a second-price, sealed-bid auction with independent private values, a player's optimal strategy is to bid his or her own valuation of the item. In fact, this is a dominant strategy.

26. In a first-price, sealed-bid auction with independent private values, a bidder's optimal strategy is to bid less than his or her valuation of the item. If there are n bidders who all perceive valuations to be evenly (or uniformly) distributed between a lowest possible valuation of L and a highest possible valuation of H, then the optimal bid for a player whose own valuation is v is given by

$$b = v - \frac{v - L}{n},$$

where b denotes the player's optimal bid.

27.   With independent private values, revenue equivalence holds: the auctioneer's expected revenues are the same for all four auction types.

28.   With affiliated value estimates the auctioneer earns greater expected revenues in an English auction than a second-price auction, and the lowest expected revenues in a first-price or Dutch auction.

Questions: Chapter 12

1.   There is a 90 percent chance that an investment will yield a payoff of $100, and a 10 percent chance the payoff will be $200.

    a.   Calculate the mean of the random variable.

    b.   Calculate the variance.

2. A consumer wants to buy a pair of tennis shoes, and there are numerous stores that sell them. The consumer's problem, however, is that he doesn't know the prices offered by the different stores, and has to search (at a constant cost per search) at the various stores to find out. Answer the following questions based on Exhibit 12-1.

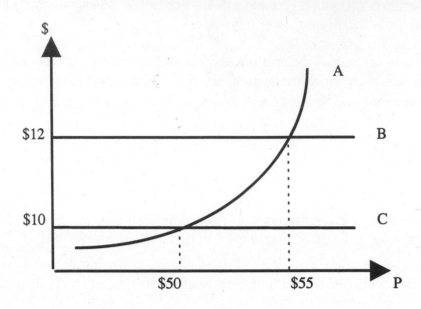

Exhibit 12-1

a. What does curve A represent?

    MB

b. What does curve B represent?

    Cost for search

c. What does curve C represent?

    cost

d. What is the consumer's reservation price if it costs $10 per search?

    $50

e. What is the consumer's reservation price if it costs $12 per search?

    $55

f. Suppose search costs are $10 per search. If the first store the consumer walks into charges $55, should the consumer purchase there or continue to search?

     Reject

212

g. Suppose search costs are $12 per search. If the first store the consumer walks into charges $50, should the consumer purchase there or continue to search?

take it

3. Determine whether the following scenarios contain adverse selection or moral hazard.

a. Joe drives fast in rental cars.

moral hazard

b. Joe loves food, and therefore always frequents "all you can eat" restaurants.

ad. selection

c. Sam gets paid a fixed $1,000 per week, and often sleeps on the job.

moral hazard

d. Joe decided to change jobs because his 12 kids need braces. He has applied to a local firm that pays the dental bills of all of its workers.

ad s l.

4. Three bidders compete in an auction for the right to purchase a U.S. Savings Bond of unknown denomination.

a. Is this a common values or independent private values situation? Explain.

b. Sam's private estimate of the Bond's value is $1,000. Should he use this estimate to form his bid? Explain.

No because of can

5. Rank the expected revenues accruing to the auctioneer in the four auction types if:

   a. Bidders are risk neutral and there are independent private valuations.

   expected same for all

   $$E = 1^{st} = 2^{nd} = D$$

   b. Bidders are risk neutral and value estimates are affiliated.

   $$E > 2^{nd} \quad \cancel{Ae} \quad 1^{st} = D$$

Technical Problems: Chapter 12

1. A risk neutral manager is attempting to buy a fleet of 15 cars. There are numerous dealers willing to sell identical fleets of cars, but different dealers charge different prices for the fleet. In fact, 1/2 of the dealers sell a 15 car fleet for $500,000 and 1/2 are willing to sell them for $450,000. The manager estimates that it costs $1,000 each time he searches another dealer.

   a. Suppose the first dealer the manager samples offers a price of $450,000. Should the manager buy the cars there, or sample another dealer?

   $$EB = \frac{1}{2}(50) + \frac{1}{2}0$$
   $$= 25,000$$

   yes

   b. Suppose the first dealer the manager samples offers a price of $500,000. Should the manager buy the cars there, or sample another dealer?

   No.

   Since EB of another firm is 25,000 SC should continue the search

2. The manager of Natural Products produces wheat flour, which is sold in a competitive market. The manager must determine how much wheat flour to produce before she knows what the market price will be. There is a 20 percent chance the market price will be $2 per pound and an 80 percent chance the market price will be $1 per pound when the wheat flour goes to market. The firm's cost function is $C = .5Q^2$.

    a.   What is the expected market price of wheat flour?

$$E = .2(2) + .8(1) = 1.2$$

    b.   What is the expected marginal revenue to the firm of selling a unit of wheat flour.

    c.   How much wheat flour should the firm produce to maximize expected profits?

$$MR = 1.2 \qquad MC = Q$$
$$1.2 = Q \qquad Q = 1.2$$

    d.   What are the firm's expected profits?

$$PQ = 1.2^2 = 1.44 - :$$
$$1.44 - .5(1.2)^2 \quad .72$$

3. You are the manager of a firm that has market power and produces at constant marginal (and average) cost of $1 per unit. There is a 50 percent chance of a recession, and a 50 percent chance of an economic boom. During a boom, the inverse demand for your product will be

$$P = 10 - .5Q.$$

If there is a recession, the inverse demand for your product will be

$$P = 6 - .5Q.$$

215

a. Is your product a normal or an inferior good?

b. What is your firm's expected marginal revenue?

c. If you are risk neutral and must set output before demand is known, how much output should you produce to maximize expected profits?

d. What is the expected price that will be charged for your product?

e. What are your expected profits?

4. You are the manager of a firm that just introduced a new product.

a. What problems might you encounter bringing your new product to market, and why?

b. Suppose your marginal cost of producing the good is under $2, and that the good is not durable. What might you do to induce customers to use your product?

c.	Would the technique you suggested in part b work if the product was a durable good? Why or why not?

d.	Now suppose the marginal cost of the product is $400, and the good is durable. Can you suggest a strategy that might induce consumers to use your product?

5.	Consider an auction where bidders have independent private values. Each bidder perceives that valuations are evenly distributed between $10 and $50. Mitchell knows his own valuation is $20. Determine Mitchell's optimal bidding strategy in

a.	a first-price, sealed-bid auction with two bidders.

$$b = V - \frac{V - L}{n}$$
$$= 20 - \frac{20 - 10}{2} = 15$$

b.	a Dutch auction with two bidders.

15

c.	a second-price sealed bid auction with 2 bidders.

20

217

Multiple Choice and True/False Questions: Chapter 12

Answer questions 1 and 2 based on the following information: Sue's search costs are $10 per search. She wants to buy a big screen TV, and the lowest price she's found so far is $1,000. Sue thinks 1/2 of the stores charge $900 for TV's and 1/2 charge $1,000. Sue's search costs are $50 per search.

S = 10
P = 1000
EB = ½ 100 = 50

1.   Sue's optimal decision is to
      a.   Continue to search for a lower price.
      b.   Stop searching and purchase a TV for $1,000.
      c.   Do either a or b, since she is indifferent between the two.

2.   If Sue's search costs increased to $100 per search she should
      a.   search less
      b.   refuse to buy a TV
      c.   search more
      d.   none of the above

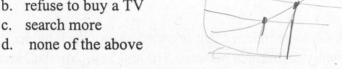

3.   Jim is offered two gambles. With gamble A, he either gains $20 or loses $20 with a 50% probability. With gamble B, he either gains $10 or loses $9 with a 50% probability. Tim prefers gamble A to gamble B. What can we conclude?
      a.   Tim is risk loving.
      b.   Tim is risk neutral.
      c.   Tim is risk averse.
      d.   insufficient information to determine

A   g>20   50%
L>20
B

4.   Which of the following statements is correct?
      a.   Information plays an important role in the economy.
      b.   Asymmetric information will generally enhance the market mechanism.
      c.   All auctions yield the same expected revenue to the seller.
      d.   None of the above are correct.

5.   Which of the following statements is true?
      a.   The Dutch and first price sealed bid auctions are strategically equivalent.
      b.   An art auction is a case of common values.
      c.   With independent private valuations, an English auction yields higher expected revenues than a second-price auction.
      d.   All of the above are true.

6. Which of the following can mitigate the problems of asymmetric information?
   a. Adverse selection.
   b. Signaling.
   c. Moral hazard.
   d. None of the above.

7. A consumer generally spends less time searching for lower prices when search costs
   a. increase.
   b. decrease.
   c. are constant.
   d. none of the above

8. Which of the following is the formula for the mean of a random variable, x, which takes on different values (x_i) with different probabilities (q_i):
   a. $Ex = q_1x_1 + q_2x_2 + ... + q_nx_n$.
   b. $Ex = (E\sqrt{x})^2$.
   c. $\sigma^2 = q_1(x_1 - Ex)^2 + q_2(x_2 - Ex)^2 + ... + q_n(x_n - Ex)^2$.
   d. none of the above.

9. Insurance companies _____ in order to reduce the undesirable effects of moral hazard.
   a. use deductibles
   b. classify clients into different types according to their histories
   c. reject the renewal of policies of those people with really bad records
   d. none of the above

10. In a second-price sealed bid auction with independent private valuations, the optimal bid of a bidder whose valuation is $20 is:
    a. $20.
    b. less than $20.
    c. greater than $20.

11. True or False: A risk-neutral competitive firm that must set output before it knows for sure the market price maximizes profits by producing where the expected output equals marginal cost.

12. True or False: In the presence of asymmetric information the market mechanism can break down.

13. True or False: Adverse selection occurs when people smoke more after buying life insurance.

14. True or False: Risk neutral persons will sometimes play gambles even if they expect, on average, to lose money by doing so.

15. True or False: The presence of insurance markets is evidence that some people are risk averse.

16. True or False: After a person buys insurance for his car, he will generally not care for his car as much as he otherwise would. This is an example of moral hazard.

17. True or False: People having a bad driving record find it difficult to buy automobile insurance because insurance companies fear that adverse selection will occur if they raise the premiums.

18. True or False: To avoid the winner's curse, a bidder should revise downward his private estimate of the value of the item in a common values auction.

19. True or false: With independent private valuations, bidders need to guard themselves from the winner's curse.

20. True or false: When demand is uncertain, monopolists can maximize expected profits but perfectly competitive firms can only minimize costs.

Answers to Questions: Chapter 12

1. a. $110. Calculate this as .9($100) + .1($200) = $110.

    b. 900. Calculate this as .9(100 - 110)² + .1(200 - 110)² = 900.

2. a. The expected benefit of an additional search

    b. The cost of another search when it costs $12 per search.

    c. The cost of another search when it costs $10 per search.

    d. $50. This is the point where EB = c = $10

    e. $55. This is the point where EB = c = $12

f.   Continue to search, since $55 > R = $50.

g.   Purchase there, since $50 < R = $55.

3.   a.   Moral hazard.

      b.   Adverse selection.

      c.   Moral hazard; the fixed $1,000 per week is like insurance, and induces him to reduce his effort.

      d.   Adverse selection.

4.   a.   Common values; whatever the denomination of the a U.S. savings bond, it will be worth the same amount to all bidders.

      b.   To avoid the winner's curse, Sam should revise down his private estimate.

5.   a.   English = First Price = First Price = Dutch.

      b.   English > Second Price > Dutch = First Price.

Answers to Technical Problems: Chapter 12

1.   a.   Buy there. It costs $1,000 to sample another dealer, and the manager has already found the lowest price in the market. Continuing to search only wastes money.

      b.   Sample another dealer. The expected benefits of continuing to search are EB = .5($500,000 - $450,000) + .5(0) = $25,000. Since EB > c = $1,000, the manager should continue to search until it finds a dealer willing to sell a fleet for $450,000.

2.   a. $1.20. Compute this as EP = .2($2) + .8($1) = $1.2.

      b. $1.20. Since this firm is perfectly competitive, E(MR) = EP = $1.20.

221

c. 1.2 units. To see this, note that MC = Q. Set E(MR) = MC to get 1.20 = Q, or Q = 1.2 units.

d. .72. Compute this as $E(P) \times Q - C(Q) = (\$1.2)(1.2) - .5(1.2)^2 = .72$.

3. a. A normal good. Note that demand is higher during a boom than during a recession.

    b. E(MR) = 8 - Q. Notice that during a boom your MR is $MR_B = 10 - Q$, while it is $MR_R = 6 - Q$ during a recession. Hence, E(MR) = .5(10 - Q) + .5(6 - Q) = 8 - Q.

    c. 7 units. To see this, set E(MR) = MC to get 8 - Q = 1, or Q = 7 units.

    d. $4.5. To see this, note that the expected inverse demand is EP = .5(10 - .5Q) + .5(6 - .5Q) = 8 - .5Q. Thus, when Q = 7, EP = 8 - .5(7) = $4.5.

    e. $24.50. Compute this as ($4.5)(7) - 7 = $24.5.

4. a. Risk averse consumers will be hesitant to use the product, unless they are compensated for the risk associated with trying it.

    b. For a low-cost non-durable good, free samples might be a reasonable strategy. You might even try advertisements. It's unlikely that a money back guarantee on a low ticket item will insure them against the risk of trying it; the transactions costs to them of getting their money back probably wouldn't be worth the hassle, and therefore the offer wouldn't provide any insurance.

    c. A free sample wouldn't work well if the product is a durable good. Once you give them one for free, even if they liked it they wouldn't have an incentive to buy another one.

    d. For a big ticket durable item, a money back guarantee would provide some insurance against risk and therefore might induce them to try your product. You might also try advertisements directed at demonstrating product quality.

5.   a.   With only two bidders, $n = 2$. The lowest possible valuation is $L = \$10$, and Mitchell's own valuation is $v = \$20$. Thus, Mitchell's optimal sealed bid is

$$b = v - \frac{v - L}{n} = 20 - \frac{20 - 10}{2} = \$15$$

    b.   Since a Dutch auction is strategically equivalent to a first-price, sealed-bid auction, we can use that formula to determine the price at which Mitchell should declare his willingness to buy the item. Here, $n = 2$, the lowest possible valuation is $L = \$10$, and Mitchell's own valuation is $v = \$20$. Thus,

$$b = v - \frac{v - L}{n} = 20 - \frac{20 - 10}{2} = \$15$$

        Mitchell's optimal strategy is to let the auctioneer continue to lower the price until it reaches $15, and then yell "Mine!"

    c.   Mitchell should bid his true valuation, which is $20.

Answers to Multiple Choice and True/False Questions:
Chapter 12

1.   c
2.   a
3.   a
4.   a
5.   a
6.   b
7.   a
8.   a
9.   a

10.   a
11.   False; $E(P) = MC$.
12.   True
13.   False; moral hazard
14.   False
15.   True
16.   True
17.   True
18.   True
19.   False; the winner's curse occurs in a common value auction.
20.   False; both can maximize expected profits.

Chapter 13
A Manager's Guide to Government in the Marketplace

Chapter 13 at a Glance

Key Concepts: Chapter 13

1.   Four factors sometimes keep a free market from providing the socially efficient quantities of goods:
    a.   market power
    b.   externalities
    c.   public goods
    d.   incomplete information.

2.   A firm has market power when it sells output at a price that exceeds its marginal cost of production.

3.   Antitrust policy attempts to eliminate the deadweight loss of monopoly by making it illegal for managers to engage in activities that foster monopoly power, such as price-fixing agreements and other collusive practices.

4.   Under the 1984 merger guidelines (revised in 1997), a merger may be challenged if:

    a.   The HHI in an industry is greater than 1800, or would be after merger; or if

    b.   The HHI is between 1000 and 1800, the merger is to be carefully examined.

5.   In the presence of large economies of scale, it may be desirable for a single firm to service a market. In these instances, government may allow a firm to exist as a monopoly, but choose to regulate its price in order to reduce the deadweight loss.

6.   The Antitrust Division of the Department of Justice (DOJ) and the Federal Trade Commission (FTC) are charged with the task of enforcing antitrust regulations.

7.   The *Hart-Scott-Rodino Antitrust Improvement Act* of 1976 requires that parties to an acquisition notify both the DOJ and the FTC of their intent to merge, provided that the dollar value of the acquisition exceeds a certain threshold.

8.   Some production processes create costs for people who are not part of the production or consumption process for the good.   These external costs are called negative externalities.

9.   In the presence of externalities, a free market will generally fail to produce the socially efficient amount of the good.

10. The Clean Air Act causes firms to internalize the cost of emitting pollutants, since a fee must be paid for each unit emitted. This raises each firm's marginal cost and therefore induces them to produce less output.

11. A good is non-rival in consumption if the consumption of the good by one person does not preclude other people from also consuming the good.

12. A good or service is non-exclusionary if, once it is provided, no one can be excluded from consuming the good or service.

13. A good is public if it is non-exclusionary and non-rival in consumption.

14. Government policies will generally benefit some parties at the expense of others. For this reason, lobbyists spend considerable sums of money in attempts to affect government policies. This process is known as rent-seeking.

15. The purpose of a quota is to limit the number of units of a product that foreign competitors can bring into the country. This reduces competition in the domestic market, which results in higher prices, higher profits for domestic firms, and lower consumer surplus for domestic consumers.

16. Tariffs are fees imposed on foreign imports, and are designed to limit foreign competition in the domestic market. Tariffs benefit domestic producers at the expense of domestic consumers and foreign producers.

17. A lump sum tariff is a fixed fee that foreign firms must pay the domestic government in order to be able to sell in the domestic market.

18. A per unit (excise) tariff requires the importing firms to pay the domestic government a fee on each unit they bring into the country.

19. A lump sum tariff does not shift up the marginal cost curve of foreign producers, but it does reduce the profits of foreign firms. It only benefits domestic producers if the lump sum tariff is so high that it induces foreign firms to exit the domestic market.

20. An excise tariff shifts the marginal cost curve for foreign firms shifts up by the amount of the tariff, which in turn decreases the supply of all foreign firms.

Questions: Chapter 13

1. List the four major sources of market failure, and explain how each leads to market failure.

    a.

    b.

    c.

    d.

2. Explain two ways the government attempts to alleviate the problems associated with market power.

    a.

    b.

3. List five ways the government attempts to alleviate the problems associated with incomplete information.

    a.

b.

c.

d.

e.

4.   Answer the following questions based on Exhibit 13-1.

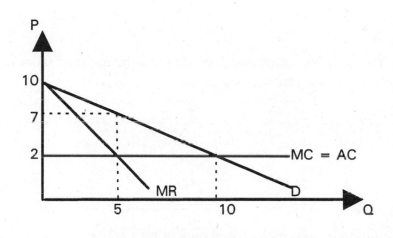

Exhibit 13-1

a.   What is the deadweight loss of this monopoly?

b.   Suppose the government imposes a price ceiling of $2. How will this affect the deadweight loss?

c.   How much will the monopolist be willing to spend to avoid the price regulation?

d.   How much will all consumers be willing to spend to lobby for the price regulation?

e.   Suppose there are 1,000 consumers in this market. How much will the average consumer gain if the price regulation is imposed?

f.   If there are 1,000 consumers, do you think the monopolist or the consumers are likely to win the rent seeking endeavor?

5.   Answer the following questions based on Exhibit 13-2.

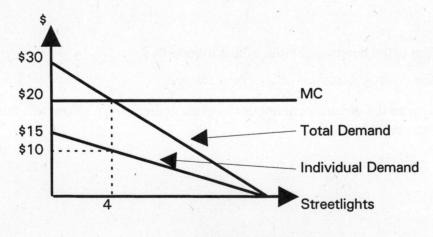

Exhibit 13-2

a.   How many individuals desire the public good?

b.   How much would it cost to provide 4 streetlights?

c.   Would an individual consumer be willing to pay for a streetlight?

d.   What is the socially efficient number of streetlights?

e.   How much would each consumer have to pay in order for the efficient number of streetlights to be provided?

f.   How much consumer surplus does each consumer receive if the efficient number of streetlights are provided and each individual is required to pay the efficient amount?

Technical Problems: Chapter 13

1.   Suppose the external marginal cost of producing steel is

$$MC_{External} = 2Q,$$

while the internal marginal cost is

$$MC_{Internal} = Q.$$

Further assume the inverse demand for steel is given by

$$P = 10 - Q.$$

a.   What is the socially efficient level of output?

b.   How much output would a competitive industry produce?

2.   A town has 4 residents, all of which desire a larger police force. Each resident has an inverse demand for police services of

$$P = 10 - Q,$$

where Q is the number of hours of police services. The marginal cost of hiring a policeman is $20 dollars per hour.

a.   Do you think police services are a public good? Explain.

b.   What is the total demand for police services?

c.   What is the socially efficient number of hours of police services?

d.   How much would each person have to pay per hour of services in order to achieve the efficient quantity?

3.   You are the manager of a monopoly that faces an inverse demand curve

$$P = 5 - Q,$$

and has a cost function

$$C(Q) = Q.$$

The government is considering legislation that would regulate your price at the competitive level.

a.   What is the maximum amount you would be willing to spend on legal lobbing activities designed to stop the regulation?

b.   How much would all consumers, taken together, be willing to spend to lobby in favor of the regulation?

4.   Suppose the supply of a good by domestic firms is

$$Q^{SD} = 10 + P,$$

and the supply by foreign firms is

$$Q^{SF} = 10 + P.$$

The domestic demand for the product is given by

$$Q^d = 30 - P.$$

a.   Find the equation for the total supply of the good provided in the domestic market.

b.   What is the equilibrium price of the good?

c.   Suppose a quota of 1 unit is imposed on foreign producers. Find the equilibrium price under the quota.

5.   Answer the following questions based on Exhibit 13-3, which assumes the market is initially in equilibrium at point A, where total foreign and domestic supply equals domestic demand.

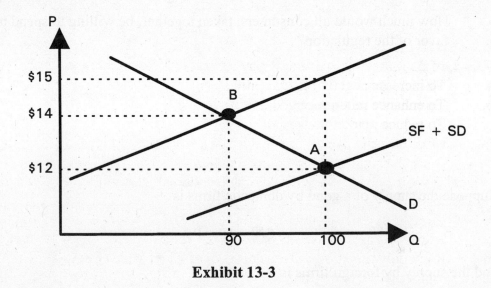

Exhibit 13-3

a. What is the equilibrium price in the domestic market?

b. What is the equilibrium quantity in the domestic market?

c. If a $3 per unit tariff is imposed on foreign producers, what happens to the equilibrium price?

d. If a $3 per unit tariff is imposed on foreign producers, what happens to the equilibrium quantity?

e. Do domestic consumers benefit from the tariff?

f. Do domestic firms benefit from the tariff?

Multiple Choice and True/False Questions: Chapter 13

1. Which of the following is a role of government in a free market society?
   a. To increase negative externalities.
   b. To enhance rent-seeking activities.
   c. To reduce market power.
   d. None of the above.

2. Which of the following is not true of markets that involve negative externalities in production?
   a. Competitive firms produce more than the efficient level of output.
   b. Society gains because firms do not pay the external costs of production.
   c. Monopoly might provide the socially efficient level of output.
   d. All of the above are true.

3.   Which of the following is not a public good?
      a.   national defense
      b.   streetlights
      c.   Cable TV
      d.   all of the above are public goods

4.   When the government imposes a lump sum tariff on foreign imports:
      a.   marginal cost shifts up by the amount of the tax.
      b.   profits of foreign firms fall.
      c.   all of the above.
      d.   none of the above.

5.   In the absence of price regulation, firms with market power charge prices
      a.   below MC.
      b.   above MR
      c.   above MC
      d.   (b) and (c)

6.   Which of the following is true for a monopoly?
      a.   A monopoly always makes a positive profit.
      b.   A price ceiling on a monopoly always reduces its output.
      c.   A price ceiling on a monopoly always increases its output.
      d.   None of the above are true.

7.   With a negative externality in production, the internal marginal cost
      a.   exceeds the social marginal cost.
      b.   exceeds the external marginal cost.
      c.   is less than the social marginal cost.
      d.   is less than the external marginal cost.

8.   A firm has a constant marginal social cost of producing that equals $2, and a constant internal cost of producing that equals $1. What is the socially efficient level of production for a firm facing an inverse demand $P = 10 - Q$?
      a.   2
      b.   7
      c.   8
      d.   9

9.	The domestic demand for a good is $Q^d = 40 - P$. The domestic supply is $Q^{SD} = 3P$, while the foreign supply is $Q^{SF} = 10P$. What is the equation for the total supply of the good in the domestic market?
	a.	$Q = 3P$
	b.	$Q = 7P$
	c.	$Q = 13P$
	d.	$Q = 30P$

10.	True or False: A price ceiling imposed on a monopoly may lead to a shortage of the good.

11.	True or False: In general, consumers taken as a whole stand to gain more from regulating a monopolist's price than the monopolist stands to lose.

12.	True or False: In order to eliminate the inefficiency brought about by a monopoly, the government can simply regulate price at the competitive level, unless that price is below ATC.

13.	True or False: If the government imposes a price ceiling below the monopolist's average cost curve, then in the long run the monopolist will go out of business unless it receives a subsidy from the government.

14.	True or False: The external marginal cost measures the cost to society of producing a good.

15.	True or False: In the presence of production externalities, the social marginal cost equals the sum of internal and external marginal costs.

16.	True or False: In general, free markets do not provide the efficient level of public goods.

17.	True or False: In general, excise tariffs imposed on foreign imports raise the prices domestic consumers pay for goods.

18.	True or False: Laws against insider trading are designed to alleviate the problems of public goods in securities markets.

19.	True or False: The "free rider problem" refers to the fact that individuals have little private incentive to pay for the provision of public goods.

20.	True or False: "Rent seeking" refers to attempts by consumers to pay low housing costs in markets dominated by insiders.

Answers to Questions: Chapter 13

1. a. Market power. In the absence of externalities, it results in prices in excess of the marginal social cost of the good, and thus too little output.

    b. Externalities. Negative externalities in production lead to too much output, because firms ignore the external costs to society of production.

    c. Public goods. Because of the nonrival and nonexclusionary nature of these goods, individuals have an incentive to "free ride", that is, to let others pay for the goods. This leads to the under provision of public goods.

    d. Incomplete information. When consumers have incomplete information about the attributes of goods, they cannot generally make optimal decisions. Furthermore, asymmetric information can entirely destroy a market.

2. a. Antitrust laws. These are designed to keep firms from obtaining or exerting excessive market power.

    b. Price regulation. These are designed to force firms with market power to charge socially efficient prices, and thereby to produce socially efficient quantities of goods.

3. a. Rules against insider trading

    b. Certification

    c. Truth in lending

    d. Truth in advertising

    e. Enforcing contracts

4. a. $12.50. A monopolist produces 5 units, and charges a price of $7. Therefore, the area of the deadweight triangle is .5(10 - 5) x ($7 - $2) = $12.5.

    b. With a ceiling price of $2, the monopolist produces 10 units of output. Therefore, the deadweight loss is zero.

    c. Up to $25. In the absence of the ceiling, the monopolist produces 5 units to earn profits of ($7 - $2) x 5 = $25 dollars. Since it stands to make zero profits if the regulation is imposed, it is willing to spend up to this amount in lobbying expenditures to avoid the price regulation.

d. Up to $37.50. Consumers stand to gain additional surplus equal to the monopoly profits ($25) plus the deadweight loss ($12.50). Thus, all consumers taken together will be willing to spend up to $37.50 lobbying for the price regulation.

e. Less than 4 cents. The total surplus of all consumers is $37.50, so the average surplus of a consumer is $37.50/1,000 = $0.0375, which is less than four cents.

f. The monopolist, since it stands to lose much more than any single consumer would gain. Even the cost of a postage stamp exceeds the value to a consumer of successfully lobbying, so it is doubtful that consumers would even write their representative.

5. a. 2. To see this, note that the total demand for streetlights is twice as high as the individual demand for streetlights, so there must be two individuals.

b. $80. The marginal cost of a streetlight is $20, so 4 would cost $80.

c. No. Notice that the vertical intercept of the individual demand for streetlights is $15, indicating that even if no streetlights are available, an individual would only be willing to pay $15 for the first streetlight. This is less than the cost of providing each streetlight ($20).

d. 4. This occurs where the total demand for streetlights equals MC.

e. $40. Each consumer pays $10 per streetlight, for a total cost of $40.

f. $10. This is computed as .5($15 - $10) x 4 = $10.

Answers to Technical Problems: Chapter 13

1. a. 2.5 units. Note that $MC_{Social} = MC_{External} + MC_{Internal} = 2Q + Q = 3Q$. Equate this with price to get $3Q = 10 - Q$, or $Q = 2.5$ units, the socially efficient level.

b. 5 units. A competitive industry ignores external costs, and therefore produces where $MC_{Internal} = P$, or $Q = 10 - Q$. Solving for Q gives us $Q = 5$.

2.   a.   Yes, to some extent. If a policeman is protecting your neighbor's house, you will benefit too. Thus, there is an element of non-exclusion. Further, there is non-rival consumption in the sense that so long as the policeman is in the neighborhood, he can watch several houses at the same time. However, the policeman might actually have difficulty stopping two crimes at the same time.

      b. $P_{Total} = 4(10 - Q) = 40 - 4Q$. This is the total amount that all four consumers would pay for Q hours of police services.

      c.   5 hours. Equate the total demand with marginal cost to get $40 - 4Q = 20$. Solving for Q gives us $Q = 5$ hours.

      d. $5. Plug $Q = 5$ into the individual demand to get $P = 10 - 5 = \$5$.

3.   a.   Up to $4. A monopolist will spend up to its profits to avoid having to charge marginal cost. To calculate monopoly profits, notice that $MR = 5 - 2Q$. Setting this equal to marginal cost ($MC = 1$) give us $5 - 2Q = 1$. Solving for Q gives us $Q^M = 2$. The monopoly price is $P^M = 5 - 2 = \$3$. Therefore, monopoly profits are $P^M \times Q^M - C(Q^M) = \$3 \times 2 - (2) = \$4$.

      b.   Up to $6. Consumers will spend up to the amount they will gain in consumer surplus as a result of getting to pay a price equal to marginal cost. Since marginal cost is constant, this gain equals the monopolist's profits, plus the deadweight loss. To compute the deadweight loss, note that a competitive industry would produce where $P = MC$, or $5 - Q = 1$. Solving for Q gives us $Q^C = 4$ units. Notice that since marginal cost is constant, the deadweight loss under monopoly is $.5(P^M - MC) \times (Q^C - Q^M) = .5(\$3 - \$1) \times (4 - 2) = \$2$. Thus, the sum of monopoly profits ($4) plus the deadweight loss ($2) is what consumers stand to gain.

4.   a. $Q^{Total} = 20 + 2P$. This is obtained computing $Q^{SD} + Q^{SF}$.

      b. $3.33. To see this, set $Q^{Total} = Q^d$ to get $20 + 2P = 30 - P$. Solving for P gives us $P = 3\ 1/3$.

      c. $9.50. With a quota, total supply is the domestic supply, plus the quota of 1 unit by foreign firms, or $Q^{Total} = 10 + P + 1 = 11 + P$. Setting this equal to domestic demand gives us $11 + P = 30 - P$. Solving for P we get $P = \$9.50$.

5.   a. $12. This is the price corresponding to point A.

      b.   100 units. This is the quantity corresponding to point A.

c. It rises to $14, a $2 increase. Notice that supply shifts up by the amount of the tariff, resulting in a new equilibrium at point B. The price is only $2 higher at B compared to point A, even though the tariff shifted supply up by $3.

d. It falls to 90 units. This corresponds to point B.

e. Domestic consumers receive fewer goods and pay higher prices, so they are harmed. Their lost consumer surplus is $10, computed as .5($14-$12) (100-90) = $10.

f. Domestic producers benefit because they can sell their output at a higher price and produce more output, due to the effect of the tariff.

Answers to Multiple Choice and True/False Questions:
Chapter 13

1. c
2. b
3. c
4. b
5. d
6. d
7. c
8. c
9. c
10. True
11. True
12. True
13. True
14. False; social marginal cost measures this
15. True
16. True
17. True
18. False; to alleviate the problems of asymmetric information
19. True
20. False